y Punishment

...d comforting way of discussing a misunderstood and isolating illness. Reading it was like sitting in an overstuffed couch talking to a best friend. It gives hope to those suffering with OCD but also those with loved ones with OCD that they can't 'understand.' Wonderful read. I did not put it down until I read it cover to cover!"

Lisa I. Carroll
Supervising US Probation Officer, Middle District of Louisiana

"Sarcastic, witty, insightful! Maggie Lamond Simone writes with a sincerity that is endearing and frank, giving a voice to the internal conversations that lead to silent suffering for many. *Body Punishment* is an insight into the life and mind of an innocent being conditioned by OCD—colorful, dramatic, passionate, sharp, and disruptive at times, though beautiful when seeing it as a whole."

Kaushal B. Nanavati, MD, FAAFP, ABIHM
Director, Integrative Medicine, Upstate Cancer Center
Assistant Professor, Department of Family Medicine
SUNY Upstate Medical University

"Maggie Simone provides a deeply personal account of her experiences with OCD and addiction. She shows how one can overcome significant psychiatric challenges while leading a productive, fulfilling life."

Kevin P. Hill, MD, MHS
Assistant Professor of Psychiatry
McLean Hospital/Harvard Medical School

"*Body Punishment* is a deeply personal account of living with OCD. Maggie recounts her childhood and how undiagnosed OCD impacted her self-esteem and life experiences. Maggie's open, honest, and humorous writing style allows the reader an unusually intimate glimpse into the life of someone living with OCD.

"She chronicles the evolution of addiction from self-medicating to alleviate symptoms of anxiety to the point where alcohol use takes on a life of its own. Her life example offers hope, empathy, and a sense of belonging for someone with OCD.

"*Body Punishment* is a compelling read and one we will recommend to our clients."

Cary Rector, MS, LMHC
Tonja Rector, MA, LMFT

"*Body Punishment* is remarkably intimate and inspiring. Maggie Lamond Simone bares her soul in a way that can only be described as beautifully vulnerable.

"Correlating her experiences in the martial arts with her growing realization about her mental illness and alcoholism, she brilliantly exposes both as journeys of insight, healing, and personal growth. This book creates an opening for those who struggle with any mental affliction; through her courageous self-disclosures, Simone lets others know they are not alone, that they can be empowered to act, and, perhaps most importantly, there is no shame in mental illness."

Dr. William A. Raineri, Orthodontist
Fourth Degree Black Belt

BODY PUNISHMENT

BODY PUNISHMENT

OCD, ADDICTION, AND FINDING THE COURAGE TO HEAL

MAGGIE LAMOND SIMONE

CENTRAL RECOVERY PRESS

LAS VEGAS

Central Recovery Press (CRP) is committed to publishing exceptional materials addressing addiction treatment, recovery, and behavioral healthcare topics, including original and quality books, audio/visual communications, and web-based new media. Through a diverse selection of titles, we seek to contribute a broad range of unique resources for professionals, recovering individuals and their families, and the general public.

For more information, visit www.centralrecoverypress.com.

Publisher: Central Recovery Press
              3321 N. Buffalo Drive
              Las Vegas, NV 89129

20 19 18 17 16 15   1 2 3 4 5

ISBN: 978-1-937612-81-8 (paper)
      978-1-937612-82-5 (e-book)

Photo of Maggie Lamond Simone by Katrina Grady

Publisher's Note: This is a memoir, a work based on fact recorded to the best of the author's memory. Central Recovery Press books represent the experiences and opinions of their authors only. Every effort has been made to ensure that events, institutions, and statistics presented in our books as facts are accurate and up-to-date. To protect their privacy, the names of some of the people and institutions in this book may have been changed.

This book contains general information about OCD, alcoholism, and suggested treatments. The information is not medical advice, and should not be treated as such. Central Recovery Press makes no representations or warranties in relation to the medical information in this book; this book is not an alternative to medical advice from your doctor or other professional healthcare provider. If you have any specific questions about any medical matter you should consult your doctor or other professional healthcare provider. If you think you or someone close to you may be suffering from any medical condition, you should seek immediate medical attention. You should never delay seeking medical advice, disregard medical advice, or discontinue medical treatment because of information in this or any book.

Cover design, interior design, and layout by Sara Streifel, Think Creative Design

This book is dedicated to my parents, who,
with little of the knowledge available today about
what goes on in our heads and why,
never lost sight of their love for us.

I'm hoping one day my children
will say the same about me.

CONTENTS

FOREWORD

People who live with obsessive-compulsive disorder experience severe anxiety. They have persistent, intrusive, and unwanted thoughts and urges that interfere with their daily lives. The obsessive thoughts lead them to the compulsive behaviors. As a society, we tend to overuse the term "OCD"—for example, when we share a story and say, "I'm a bit OCD when it comes to my closet." That is not OCD, unless you can't leave your closet for hours on end, in which case you may need some help. "OCD" is not an adjective. It is a commonly misunderstood illness. Family members may chalk up the symptoms they see in loved ones to "quirks" and not recognize how debilitating it is.

People who suffer from OCD can go undiagnosed for their entire lives due, in large part, to the guilt, shame, and embarrassment they feel in relationship to the illness. The *Diagnostic and Statistical Manual of Mental Disorders* (DSM) has recognized certain similarities among a variety of anxiety-driven conditions; the latest edition, 2013's *DSM-5*, has reclassified them under the umbrella heading of "obsessive-compulsive disorders." These disorders include trichotillomania (hair-pulling), as well as excoriation (skin-picking). Maggie's candor in disclosing her thoughts and feelings pertaining specifically to these issues will open many people's eyes to the "body punishment" that is related to OCD.

OCD is a chronic, anxiety-based illness that can be managed through therapy and with medication. Behavior therapy is the most common form of treatment in an outpatient setting. Therapy and medication reduce the symptoms of OCD; however, the struggle remains for most, as the intrusive thoughts and unwanted urges can linger. The intelligent self understands that the thoughts and behaviors are irrational and unnecessary but simply cannot turn off the fear that urges a person to complete a ritual. It takes a great deal of self-awareness and sheer will to ignore the fears that are driving the obsessive thoughts.

> "The French once called OCD *la folie de doute*, which translates to the 'doubting disease.' Doubt is one of the emotions that feeds most obsessive and compulsive behavior and it is this inability to live with doubt and uncertainty that drives OCD. People with OCD prefer black or white answers for their OCD, rather than being able to accept shades of grey."
>
> From OCD-UK, www.ocduk.org

The root cause of OCD is unknown; the belief is that there are changes in functioning of brain pathways involved with planning, judgment, and body movements. Environmental influences, such as familial relationships or stressful events, also have an impact. There is also evidence that the chemical imbalance related to serotonin can be inherited; however, the symptoms are so varied and seemingly disparate that a parent's manifestations could be much different than her child's.

So often these issues go untreated due to the shame so many feel about the behaviors Maggie writes about. These issues leave a person feeling isolated and alone and fearful of anyone learning their truth; the effects on a young child's self-esteem are staggering. But the truth is that in learning to acknowledge and speak about their struggles with a professional, relief can be found.

Maggie's writing allows readers to truly have a view from the inside out. Parents and loved ones of anyone suffering from these symptoms would greatly benefit from reading this book, as so many of the people I work with struggle to understand how their loved one can "do these things to themselves." They are some of the most difficult for someone with OCD to overcome and the most difficult for outsiders to comprehend.

Readers who suffer from OCD will find relief in knowing they are not alone. So many of my clients who suffer in these ways cannot believe anyone else possibly thinks the way they think or does the things they do. The world of OCD is isolating and this book can change that for the reader. Maggie's honesty and determination can offer someone hope when he or she feels there is none.

I encourage anyone who is struggling with OCD or knows someone who is to read this book and share it with others. Maggie's bold, compelling, witty charm is so honest and brave you won't be able to put it down.

Kelly E. Hamilton, LMHC, BCC
Licensed Mental Health Counselor
Baldwinsville, New York

ACKNOWLEDGMENTS

This book would not have been possible without the patience and understanding (always attempted, often achieved) of my husband and children. I spent many weekends writing in hotels because my home is such a place of peace and contentment that I found it impossible, under its roof, to evoke the feelings and memories I wanted to convey. I want to thank them, as well, for their perpetual support of my need for transparency—my mission to eliminate shame and stigma has often exposed them as well, and they've remained by my side . . . often without complaint. Ha! Kidding. They're my biggest fans.

I want it to be perfectly clear that nothing in this book is intended as an indictment of the people and events that occurred. The sharing of those events was for the sole purpose of conveying the depths and extent of my own issues, and the impact of the shame of mental illness on my daily life experiences. In fact, many of those people and events contributed to my survival and eventual ability to get help, for which I am truly indebted to them.

I want to thank Ermine Cunningham, Linda Lowen, Laurel McHargue, and Marcia Hafner, tasked not only with reading an unedited manuscript but reading *this* unedited manuscript.

Your feedback was invaluable. Thank you as well to the mother-daughter team of Ellen Yeomans and Alex Arnold, whose insights brought the manuscript back to life after it had gotten comfortable on a shelf. My parents, my brothers, my sister, my amazing friends—you've watched me live with the issues in this book and you love me anyway. Thank you for that. And you supported my need to bring them to light . . . thank you for that as well.

My agent, Dana Newman, and Nancy Schenck, Valerie Killeen, and Daniel Kaelin at CRP—your belief in the value of my story gave me a sense of validation that I couldn't seem to give myself. Thank you.

PROLOGUE

I remember watching my very first black belt exam after I'd had my introductory karate class. I was with a friend who had begun a few months prior, and she explained all of the moves they were doing throughout the session. It was exciting to watch, very energetic and technical and almost spiritual, and I was beginning to think that maybe I wouldn't be able to do it. It was very graceful, very choreographed, and, typically, I wasn't known for my grace or choreography. Suddenly, however, I was riveted.

The black belt candidates lined up side by side, with their legs bent and slightly spread apart and their fists tucked against their ribs: the traditional "horse stance." There was total silence in the gym. As I watched, transfixed, the upper-degree black belts lined up facing the candidates and started making their way down the line and, one by one, punching them in the stomach as hard as they could. The air was now punctuated by shouts and grunts and "*ay-yah!'s*," and I finally asked my friend, "What the hell are they doing?"

She replied, "It's called body punishment. When you're training for your black belt, you learn how to concentrate and breathe in such a way that you can absorb a blow to the stomach."

"Do you mean they're lining up to see how many hits they can take?" I asked, incredulous.

"Well, yes, in a way," she said. "It's basically to test your focus but also, I guess, to see how much you can take."

"Okay," I said. "Just so I understand, the goal is to get as hurt as you can without showing that you're hurt?"

My friend looked at me curiously. "Well, yes, I guess," she said.

I thought about all of the ways I'd hurt myself throughout the years that I hid in shame, and the ways I'd hurt myself that couldn't be hidden and were, therefore, a source of even greater shame. I thought about the years I'd spent silently wondering what was wrong with me that compelled me, from childhood, to do these things to myself no matter how hard I tried to stop. I thought about the parts of my life that I'd lost to alcohol because self-medicating was my only escape from the mental torture with which I'd suffered privately since I was old enough to step over a crack.

I watched those black belt candidates lined up on the floor, waiting to get punched in the stomach by fifteen other people, hoping to be congratulated and promoted to black belt when it was over.

I said, "Oh, yes. This is the sport for me."

CHAPTER ONE
WHITE BELT

"WHITE, THE COLOR OF A SEEDLING BENEATH THE COVER OF EARTH, SIGNIFIES A BEGINNER TO THE MARTIAL ARTS. WHITE ALSO SYMBOLIZES THE INNOCENCE OF A NEW STUDENT WHO EMBARKS ON HIS JOURNEY WITH NO PRIOR KNOWLEDGE."

~GWEN BRUNO, LIVESTRONG.COM

When I first joined karate a few weeks before my thirtieth birthday, I was afraid of many things—trying something new, trying it without knowing anybody, looking like an idiot, sweating, not being able to physically do what I was expected to do—but what I was not afraid of was yelling. Until I realized I couldn't do it.

In my karate school, it was called "breathing," but whatever they termed it, I couldn't do it. I could not yell on command. Every punch, every kick was supposed to be accompanied by a "*tee-ya!*" or an "*ay-yah!*" that would make the move more powerful. And I couldn't do it. So much of my life had been spent shutting up, being quiet, blending in, going along to get along, that I was physically unable to shout.

It was months before I let that first "*tee-ya!*" fly and realized that the world was not going to fall apart around me simply because I opened my mouth.

1998, AGE THIRTY-SIX.

As I lie completely still in the very close and very loud banging and pinging quarters of an MRI machine, I'm struck by two thoughts: First, that I'll probably never lose the image of being stuffed inside an empty paper towel roll, and second, that I'm not nearly as claustrophobic as I thought I would be. Give me headphones and some good music and I can lie in a tube forever.

I'm in here for a battery of tests to determine once and for all the root of my almost daily headaches, vertigo, and short-term memory loss. All of these symptoms are explained by my history of migraines, but my doctor wants to make sure there's nothing else going on—inner ear trouble, sinus problems gone awry, anything that could affect balance—before I start a daily migraine treatment. I'm looking forward to that treatment, I tell her, because the migraines have been debilitating in the six years I've been suffering from them, and because, now that I have children, I harbor a secret paranoia of being remembered by them—and described in passing by generations to come—like a "delicate" mom from the eighteenth century who was forever retiring to her quarters with her "spells."

My other secret, however, is a little more perverse. I'm actually kind of, sort of, a little bit hoping there's a brain tumor somewhere in there, or some disease—curable, of course—that would help to explain the last thirty years' worth of bizarre behavior. Since I was a child, I've had often debilitating or paralyzing obsessive thoughts that I could not shake and rituals and compulsions that I've spent decades masking with both makeup and rationalizations, accompanied by the underlying fear that no one else has lived through what I have lived through in my head. I would certainly rest easier having a physical (as opposed to solely mental) basis for my perpetual need to self-destruct, and I'd bet on some level that my family would as well.

Then I remember. They're not even aware of it.

MY STORY BEGINS IN A PILE OF SHIT.

Literally. That is my first real memory, and it really was a pile of shit.

I have a few earlier memories, but they're sketchy, like Polaroid pictures whizzing through my brain. Seeing my first spider—a daddy longlegs, no less—in the bushes on the side of the house; the smell of the ironing my mom did on Sunday afternoons while my dad sat silently in his rocking chair watching football; the agony of laying my hand flat on the hot iron to determine if it was, in fact, hot; my mom piling us into the neighbor's car one night and driving around looking for my dad. These are the fleeting memories of the early years, when everything in my life seemed perfectly normal because there was nothing to compare it to.

I start remembering my real life in that pile of shit. Of course, I didn't know that's what it was at the time because there was grass and such growing out of it, but that's what it was. And it wasn't so much a pile as a mountain, ten feet high and twenty feet wide. A mountain of manure. Dung. Cow pies. Whatever you call it where you come from, it's all the same. Ours was a by-product of both horses and cows, since at the time both species inhabited the little slice of heaven on earth we called our backyard.

As far as my brothers and I were concerned, though, it was a real mountain, with plants and shrubs that served well as forests while our Tonka-truck-inspired imaginations did the rest.

The manure pile sat next to the barn, which was connected by a white wooden gate to a long building that housed a huge, open shed (big enough to store the hay baler in the winter); a garage with a sliding wooden door that never slid open wide enough to actually house a car; and a stable that housed the occasional cow but mostly just hay and . . . stuff—farm stuff. The shed was where we huddled to watch thunderstorms, the garage served as the backdrop to the basketball hoop (as well as home plate for my brother's catcher-to-second-base throw-out practice), and the stable served no useful purpose that I could tell.

But the barn, that was the place to be. When you stepped into that barn, the air was so thick with the smell of hay and manure and horses that you almost believed you could slice through it with your finger. When you slid open the heavy wooden door and the first shaft of sunlight beamed in, you could actually see the air: a billion little particles of dust and hay and horse breath hovering and floating, trapped by the shaft of sun that didn't let go until the door opened or closed completely.

We spent many an hour in those days walking up and down the hay baler that led up a forty-five-degree angle from the ground to the second floor of the barn. We spent many more hours on that second floor hanging from a hook, jumping off the top bale of hay, and swinging down onto the slippery, dusty, wooden floor below. For those unversed in summer farm fun, it goes like this: Once hay is baled, it is loaded onto the conveyor belt, which leads the bale to the second floor window of the barn where it is dumped off. The bales are then stacked against one side of the second floor of the barn, leaving the hook hanging down with which to retrieve the hay when needed.

We didn't do any of this work, though, because we were not farmers. We were people renting a house from farmers. When the real farmers were done baling their hay, we saw nothing on that second floor but a big, hay-filled playpen and a dangerously fun ladder leading up to it.

Unbelievably, no one was ever impaled or "de-limbed" by the hook or the hay baler; not so unbelievably, there were many sprains, splinters, cuts, bumps, and bruises. I do recall hearing the term "tetanus shot" with some regularity.

One such cut on my skinny six-year-old leg began healing with a scab that was hard and crusty over the broken skin. As I ran my fingers over it one night, I suddenly felt the need to pick it off, and I did. The pain was momentarily excruciating, and then settled into a dull, stabbing ache where the wound began bleeding again. The part of me that was mortified at what I had done was soon stomped into submission by another part of me, a part that longed to reproduce that momentary excruciating pain again and again. I was slightly disturbed by this turn of events, and way too embarrassed to tell my mother. So I didn't—for about forty years.

It was the first of many such secrets I learned to keep.

I HAVE A VERY GOOD LIFE THESE DAYS.

I'm in my fifties now, and—except for the fact that my breasts point due south, for which I blame my children—I don't look a day over . . . well, late forties. I have two kids, a husband, a dog, and three cats, all of whom I adore and who, at least today, adore me. We live in the proverbial house in the suburbs—having fled the city when my first child was old enough to run into traffic— and when I sit out in my backyard at night I can actually catch fireflies (because there are so many of them, not because I've gotten really good at it).

My resume is also impressive, at least to the casual reader: master's degree from a top journalism school, national award-winning columnist, professor, author, radio personality. As a writer, I have kind of a "big fish, little pond" thing going on where I live, and that's just fine with me. For example, when we were kids and my younger brother started playing piano better than me, I quit playing. I'm not a big fan of competition with anyone but myself. I want to be the best at what I do, and if that means doing it in a place where no one else happens to be doing it, then so be it.

Oddly enough, I don't consider myself a writer but rather a person whose only viable method of communicating is through writing. Through the years I've found redemption in admitting all of my flaws, mistakes, weaknesses, what have you—putting them on display, actually—and seeking absolution from the human race. Some such flaws are comical, and some aren't, but all of them are real. "Writer" is a lot easier to define, though, and so that's what I say I am.

At any rate, I'm in a very good place right now. As a young woman, my dreams were, in no particular order, to be a writer, to have a dog, to have a baby, and to have a cabin in Vermont. I'm three-for-four so far, and that's okay; the day's not over. Besides, I got the bonus husband in there, which, given my history of short-term commitments, wasn't even in my top five. So I've learned to be a little more flexible with the list.

I come from what I always considered a stereotypical Irish Catholic family, meaning there were plenty of kids, cousins, aunts, and uncles, as well as the attendant guilt and alcohol. My mother, father, four brothers, and sister are all alive and well, and we've stayed reasonably close personally, if not geographically. My parents have been married more than fifty years, happily for many of them; my dad, like me, is a recovering alcoholic, and the marriage certainly improved when he stopped drinking. They are my best friends. I talk to them every couple of days and drive the three hours to visit them as often as schedules permit.

And I'm a decent mother, I think. I got married late and had kids late enough in life to circumvent the stupid mistakes I could have made in my youth. Oh, sure, there was the time I broke my daughter's leg when she was six months old; those darn fluffy socks I wore should have come with a warning label: "Do not wear when walking down carpeted stairs with a child on your hip." But the cast was certainly a conversation piece, and it wasn't like she was going to remember it.

Aside from that little mishap, my family and I live a relatively pain-free existence. My kids have the benefit of grandparents and aunts and uncles and cousins, good friends, and good schools. I work from home, my husband owns his own business, and our kids are equally at ease with whichever of us is throwing the ball to them. We earn enough money to be comfortable but not so much that we've lost our sense of appreciation. The kids are healthy, smart, athletic, and often frighteningly sarcastic. They got the sarcasm from me, I suppose. Everything else probably came from their father.

When I met him, my mom gently warned me about my sarcasm, suggesting it might drive him away. She really liked him, and, in fact, one time when we broke up, toyed with the idea of taking his side. She offered the same advice when I had children, suggesting I might drive them away, despite the fact that they're essentially dependent on me until they learn to make toast, which, as far as I can tell, is not anytime in the next decade. And I try to temper the sarcasm; God help me, I do. But short of a lobotomy, there isn't much I can do. Sarcasm is my one survival tool that does not cause bodily injury, and, darn it, I'm keeping it. And besides, if that's the worst thing I pass on to them, then they should be okay.

I SIGNED UP FOR KARATE TWO WEEKS BEFORE I TURNED THIRTY.

I was single and had been in recovery one year. I had not yet discovered antidepressants and was convinced my uncontrollable mood swings and anxiety were just really bad PMS, even though

I knew many women with PMS and didn't know any who did what I did. I plucked out my eyelashes and eyebrows and picked at my face if no hair was available. An attending physician at the local psychiatric hospital had recently scolded me for an ineffective attempted suicide, apparently because my attempt had gotten him out of bed. I planned my meals around the belief that if I could just get down to skin and bones, I could start over. When I put on my karate uniform for the first time, I weighed ninety-nine pounds. One of the other women in class laughed because she couldn't pull my size zero skirt up over her thigh. My body was the most recent in a lifetime of changing and often unbearable obsessions.

From my first conscious memory, I was a perpetual outsider: a living, breathing, exposed nerve, destined through some twisted karma to feel unworthy of living at every turn. It wasn't—isn't—simply a function of feeling sorry for myself; it's a matter of truly, madly, deeply feeling that absolutely everyone else is better than me. Defining "better" gets a little tricky, particularly since by accepted standards I'm intelligent, well-educated, and often successful, but in my life, "better" has generally meant "more deserving of life."

I'd spent the vast majority of my life feeling like a freak because there couldn't possibly be anybody else on earth who did to herself what I did to myself. There couldn't be another human being who felt about herself the way I felt about myself. How someone who was so smart could feel that way, act that way, and do those things without being able to stop, I could never understand. How could I intellectually rationalize pulling out my own eyelashes? I couldn't. But if I couldn't rationalize it, then why couldn't I stop? Instead, I spent my first two decades of life searching for the solution to the indefinable void where my sense of self should have been, and the next decade pretending I didn't need it.

I've since found out, of course, that the void is no longer indefinable.

But until I found out what it was, at the embarrassingly late age of fifty-two, after taking my daughter to therapy for three years for some of the exact same manifestations, I was always looking for something to blame. If I could find it, then maybe I could fix it. Was it my childhood? If it was, how come none of my siblings did what I did? Was it self-esteem? Was it the red hair? I'd felt like an outsider since I was old enough to know what an outsider was, and I needed to know why. All the things I did—plucking out my eyelashes; picking at scabs and, later, my skin; avoiding cracks in the sidewalk when I was a kid; counting in my head until I got to a certain number, over and over again; panicking if I didn't know what time we were leaving a function, even as an adult—all of these behaviors were so random that I didn't even know where to begin to find a common thread. And so for almost forty years I thought I was simply a melting pot for crazy.

But I wasn't. Almost all of my "bizarre" behaviors were explained by one section in the latest comprehensive *Diagnostic and Statistical Manual of Mental Disorders, Fifth Edition*. What I have falls under the heading of obsessive-compulsive disorders. One term. One concept. OCD. Throw in anxiety and addiction—in my case, alcoholism—and it all falls into place. Back then, though—as a kid, through adolescence, puberty, teens, twenties, thirties—all I knew was this: I was a freak, and I was alone.

NOW I KNOW DIFFERENTLY.

There are words for all of it, I now know. And there are enough years between the worst of it and now to be able to say them out loud. Most of them, anyway.

There's the addiction; I already knew that one. There are the anorexia and bulimia; I knew those as well. As far as I know these are not considered obsessive-compulsive behaviors, although it could be argued there is an element of obsessive thought running through all of them. But under the OCD heading, besides the crack avoidance and frustrating need to count, there's also something called trichotillomania (plucking out your own hair, including eyelashes and eyebrows), or TTM, to those in the know, and something else called excoriation (compulsive skin picking, formerly known as dermatillomania—I happen to like the shorter name). They all have names. And if they have names, then I cannot possibly be the only person to have experienced them.

Yet, for almost forty years, I thought I was.

It's amazing to me that I had never previously thought to investigate why I do what I do to myself. I've always been an intelligent, resourceful woman with information at my disposal. I think the reasons are twofold: First, the obsessive thoughts and behaviors started when I was so young, and I was so ashamed of them, that I accepted them as a part of my life that I would need to hide forever; and second, I'm neither a germaphobe nor particularly organized—arguably the two most recognizable behaviors associated with OCD. Some of my compulsions were and are so distinctive as to be only recently recognized and classified as OCD. In the meantime, between the OCD and the anxiety-driven thoughts and fears, I simply thought I was a lightning rod for bizarre behavior. And I'm guessing there are still many, many people—both kids and adults—who are thinking the same thing right now and feeling very alone because of it.

That feeling of isolation has affected every aspect of my life, from work to family to marriage to children. Everything I've ever done was either impacted or driven by these obsessive thoughts and behaviors, these secrets, and the crippling insecurity of believing

I wasn't normal. It was easy to become anorexic, for example, because of my tendency toward obsessive thoughts. One day I decided I was overweight because my best friend weighed less, and—*bam!*—the OCD took care of the rest. Anorexia may not be an obsessive-compulsive disorder, but the tendency sure paves the way. OCD is a devious condition that makes you do something you don't want to do for reasons you can't understand. You try and fail repeatedly to stop and are left with the sense that you are so deeply flawed as to not be worthy of love. Or, sometimes, life.

I've always wanted to go back to find out at exactly what point in my childhood this might have kicked in. There's an overwhelming hereditary component, so I know I was born with it. Does that mean I was having the thoughts and behaviors from infancy? I sucked my thumb until I was too old to suck my thumb; I had a "crack-in-the-sidewalk" fixation at age four or five, panicking for my mother's health if by chance I couldn't avoid one. So it must have started at a reasonably young age. Unfortunately, I didn't put any of the manifestations together until I was much older, for many reasons, not the least of which was the unavailability of the Internet, invented three decades later. It's hard to research something using encyclopedias when you don't even know where to begin. It's like trying to use a dictionary to find the spelling of a word you can't spell; if you could spell it, you wouldn't need the dictionary.

I remember when one of my brothers discovered the Adult Children of Alcoholics' program and sent us all a copy of the ACOA handbook. He was thrilled to have found some validation about the impact of an alcoholic parent and wanted to make sure we all knew that our childhood experiences could be affecting our adult lives. And all I could do was look at my hairless, scarred face and starving body and think, *Oh, how nice for him.*

I was envious; he'd found his demon, and maybe now he could move on from there. Having an alcoholic parent could have been one of my demons, but it certainly wasn't the only one. I used to think that perhaps, if I discovered the origins of my self-loathing and was able to somehow come to terms with the circumstances that created it, the realization that I'd spent the majority of my life unnecessarily looking for ways to die might be hard to take; maybe *not* knowing wasn't so bad after all. Now that advances in the medical communities have revealed the OCD connection, I find I'm actually somewhat relieved.

Before that connection, however, all I could do was try to envision possible explanations for what I thought were coping mechanisms. Lack of self-esteem was the go-to excuse; I assumed that was the driving force because of the void I'd always felt, the sense of having no armor. And because I couldn't understand the underlying process, the obsessive thoughts and paralyzing anxiety, I focused instead on the results of it: anger, self-loathing, shame, fear. I also learned to internalize it all because I did not want to be a freak show in public; it's hard enough in private.

In public, I was a different person. Though privately I was desperately shy, socially awkward, and seeking to fill the void in my heart by constantly looking for love, publicly I was outgoing and discerningly dating until I found the right one. Privately, I went from apartment to apartment, job to job, career to career, searching for the place in life that would make me feel whole and normal. Publicly, I was driven: a high achiever, always seeking advancement. Even in my darkest periods I rarely went backwards in life. My sense of self-preservation always propelled me toward a better life, no matter how badly my inner turmoil tried to hold me back. I learned to pass, not unlike a gay person posing as straight, to avoid discrimination. I learned to pose—to pass—as normal.

Now I know, however. Knowledge changes many things, although not everything. For instance, while I know there are many different manifestations of OCD, I don't know when an individual's symptoms are established or even determined. Many of the obsessive-compulsive behaviors that plague me actually physically hurt, and it makes me wonder if hurting myself fulfills some kind of need. Whether it's a temporary distraction, an expression of anger, the need for physical pain to remind myself I'm alive, or a desire for punishment because I don't think I deserve to *be* alive, I do it for reasons that are valid only to me and are so secret that even I don't know what they are. And in fact, OCD doesn't need a reason.

Maybe my particular obsessive thoughts and behaviors are a way of coping with rage, whereas someone else's may help her cope with, for example, anxiety. I'm not good at expressing anger. I never have been, although with practice and patience I'm better at it today than I was forty years ago. In my family we were not encouraged to show anger as children. It was in our best interests to keep it inside and pretend that life was normal. I was very good at that, and yet I remember being so angry sometimes that I thought my head would explode—at my baby brother and sister for crying in the middle of the night when I had to get up for school in the morning; at my dad for drinking and yelling so loudly; at my mom for not making our lives better. I was angry at them, and then guilty for feeling so angry at the people I loved most, and afraid that if they knew how angry I was they wouldn't love me.

Ever since I realized I could express my feelings much more coherently with a pencil and paper I knew I would be a writer. Back then I wrote things down so my head wouldn't explode. I wrote because it gave me time to craft my emotions into acceptable, non-threatening, non-hurtful letter-form for my mother to digest.

I wrote because I was afraid that if I spoke instead, I would say things that couldn't be taken back. Writing provides the benefit of editing, and the benefit of time-induced healing before unloading one's heart. It allows us to coat our raw emotions so that they're not quite so bloody when someone else reads it.

It allowed me, again, to "pass."

So what makes people like me different from other people? I'm sure that distinction is as individual as mental disorders themselves. What I know, and I know this because I have at times experienced a fleeting normalcy and can therefore compare it to my usual state, is that I not only don't have a thick skin, it's as if I have no skin at all; I am completely exposed. Where normal people have a kind of metaphorical acrylic shell that both encases them in their own confidence and shields them from the judgment of others, I don't.

People like me have no shield, no body armor. Therefore, any negativity directed at us—real or perceived—cuts us to the bone. Every emotion is magnified, every hurt feeling amplified. And when you have no self-esteem—another casualty in the obsessive thought versus reality war—then most of the feelings we have are hurt ones. The positives can be just as powerful, but in our minds there aren't nearly as many, they're not nearly as lasting, and, on some level, they're not nearly as valid as the hurt.

Maybe this is because we don't know what to do with positive feelings, or how to hold onto them. They're not a part of the OCD cycle, which, without treatment, rules our lives. We don't have the tools to stay focused on the positive; there simply isn't room when the negative takes up all the extra space in our brains. For example, in my very first column in the local Sunday paper, I pondered whether there was a statute of limitation on eggs. The copy editor thought that didn't make sense and changed my wording to "statue of limitations," which, of course, is wrong. My very first column brought me a derisive letter from a reader asking what exactly a "statue of limitations" was and where he might find one.

After reading that letter, I couldn't get out of bed for two days.

The hundreds of glowing letters I would receive over the years that followed stayed with me for a while, but that first mean one has stayed with me for life.

HERE'S A THEORY FOR YOU.

Maybe people like me are examples of a kind of perpetual "Stockholm syndrome." Sometimes we're our own captors, sometimes it's someone else, but in order to survive we learn to bond with the people who hurt us the most. We learn to embrace our rituals and our compulsions, and to normalize them—in our own heads, at least; that way, we don't seem to hurt as much. It's kind of a stretch, yes, but sometimes that's how it feels: like captivity. It might also explain why it's so hard to seek out help sometimes; we've managed to convince ourselves that what happens is somehow completely normal. Sure, it's a kind of normal that we're too terrified to mention to any other living being, but it's a type of normal nevertheless.

I also like that little philosophical gem because it helps me understand one of the more consistent obsessive thoughts I've endured throughout my life: the belief that if I got angry, if I showed any negative emotion, if I did something that could on any level be perceived as wrong, someone would get mad at me and I would not be loved. It is paralyzing, this thought of someone being angry with me, and probably complicated—if not outright caused—by low self-esteem for which I blame the OCD. To this day, I struggle with telling someone I'm upset. I avoid confrontation and conflict like other people avoid open manholes.

And that's draining. People like me learn to hide all things negative so that others think we're fine, because fine is what other people are and we need those other people to not be mad at us.

I was a good girl and a smart girl and a nice girl, and in my head I believed I was loved for those things. All of those are good things to be, but when you feel like you *have* to be them, that your very sanity depends on it, that's a lot of pressure. On some level, I was afraid that I would not be loved for being an angry girl, a confused girl, a frightened girl, or a girl who got less than straight A's. So in the early years, I struggled to find other, socially acceptable ways to express all of those anxieties, usually through writing—journals, diaries, a column in the college newspaper. But when life became too complicated with family and school and starving and plucking, I stopped writing; it was just too hard. Instead, I took those emotions and stored them in whatever part of my brain was designed for such storage, and when it got full, well, something had to give.

Obsessive thoughts, anxiety, self-destructive behavior, abusive relationships, depression, anorexia, addiction—all are available at the fingertips of the OCD sufferer.

I only took one psychology class, so I'm guessing here about the triggers for my behaviors. But when, for example, I'm anxious, I pluck my eyebrows, and when I'm angry, I don't eat. If I have a looming public event, I pick at my skin, and if I think someone is angry with me, I am paralyzed.

And there are thousands, if not millions, of people like me who pick, pluck, use, puke, and otherwise hurt themselves in private in order to survive in public.

I KNOW THAT WHAT I'VE DONE TO MY BODY MAY HAVE REPERCUSSIONS IN THE FUTURE.

I'll never be able to drink again, for sure. I also have to watch for bone loss problems because of the anorexia. I hope that my eyebrows and lashes continue to grow back despite my omnipresent need to pluck them, but I don't know if they will. I'm reasonably sure I'll be on anti-anxiety medications for the rest of my life, and I'll probably struggle with weight issues throughout as well. Pregnancy was a challenge, for example, and I insisted on being weighed on a certain scale in the OB/GYN's office because I was convinced it read three pounds lighter than another. If someone else was using it, I would wait. If it was across the building from my exam room, I would waddle over there.

Many self-abusing behaviors are symptoms of obsessive-compulsive disorder, which can drive us to see things in the mirror that aren't there, imagine someone's anger that's not there, and handle anxiety in ways that are not healthy or anxiety-reducing. There are so many different manifestations of OCD that it's challenging sometimes to decipher one from another, or what leads to what, or what compels what. When combined with anxiety, it's almost impossible. Somewhere along the line I learned to look outside of myself for self-worth because, with the issues going on in my head, I couldn't give it to myself. I sought out men who made me feel safe and loved, then left them because of their ability to do so—a paradox it took me years to understand; I knew I wanted those feelings but could not let myself be content and satisfied with them. I didn't believe I deserved them, and so I'd start looking again. The cycle went like this: Break it off with a wonderful man under the guise of feeling smothered; meet someone else who makes me feel safe and loved; be happy for a few months, until I feel smothered; start again.

I was never happy on Christmas either, each magical morning met with a profound disappointment, to this day. And that cycle is remarkably similar: I want the perfect gift, the one that will make me feel whole, complete, but if I don't know what it is, then I can't ask for it and so I'll never get it—and so the cycle repeats.

That kind of pervasive self-doubt, the need for outside approval so that simple functionality is possible, is both exhausting and self-perpetuating. When every fiber of one's being is held together by the fine threads of other people's love and approval, it only takes one small tug to unravel the whole kit and caboodle. For some of us, one small tug can be the result of a glance misread, a phone call unreturned, a letter not received. And then the unraveling begins.

There is something about all of this—the OCD cycle of anxiety or obsessive thought, resultant compulsion, concerted effort to stop the behavior, inability to do so, resultant embarrassment and confusion, leading back to anxiety—that is so steeped in shame that I never told a soul about my issues until I was a mother and concerned for my baby. This is where public perception comes in; OCD is not just being afraid of germs and needing your cupboards organized alphabetically. The obsessive thoughts can range from intrusive to torturous, and the compulsions can be physically painful, humiliating, and dangerous. Not a lot of "cute" and "amusing" to be had in this arena, despite the Hollywood portrayals.

Sometimes it seems like we're hamsters on that little wheel. Our lack of self-worth, coupled with an overwhelming and obsessive sense of pain and futility, compels us to hurt ourselves with the compulsion *du jour*, the shame and humiliation of which simply confirms why hating ourselves is the absolutely correct thing to do, which, in turn, makes us angry, compelling us again to hurt ourselves in the compulsion *du jour*, which provides the necessary, yet painfully temporary, relief we need. The shame and humiliation of what we do in our anger again confirms our belief in our utter lack of self-worth, and the cycle continues. The obsessive-compulsive component ensures that it does.

To calm the fears of loved ones everywhere, simply reading or talking about these things—OCD, addiction, anxiety, mental illness—doesn't typically make people do something they otherwise would not do. For instance, when I first read about cutting, which I don't do, I remember thinking, *Yikes. Ouch. That's pretty harsh, don't you think?* It did not inspire me to cut. I'm many things, but I'm not a cutter. Do you see how this works? Self-abusers don't go searching for ways to self-abuse, any more than people with addiction choose what to be addicted to. I'm addicted to alcohol. I was exposed many times to drugs and had no interest in them. It's like a hard drive was installed in us when we were too young to choose our preferences.

Whatever obsessions and/or compulsions I have, I didn't choose. There are many different forms—the stereotyped organizer and germaphobe, for example. There are also hoarders, and counters, and people who have to lock and unlock their doors multiple times. There are those who repeat phrases under their breath, and people who have to go over thresholds a certain way. There are obsessive thoughts that involve hurting people we love, starting fires, horrible creatures following us. And not every obsessive thought has a corresponding compulsion; sometimes we're faced with debilitating thoughts for which there is no relief.

Obsessive thoughts and compulsive behaviors are not a conscious choice, like picking your outfit for the day would be. A closer comparison would be sleeping positions; you don't really think about sleeping on your side or your back, you just do it. Even if you try to sleep differently one night, when you wake up you're in the same position in which you usually wake up. I have never consciously thought about the things I do; I just do them. I have been drawn to them. I drew myself to them, maybe. Whatever. But I think I can put this widely-held fear to rest: Discussing OCD behaviors isn't what makes people do them any more than giving a drink to someone makes her an alcoholic. Addiction has a different basis than OCD, of course, but I feel pretty safe in saying neither is caused by knowledge.

Also, not unlike addiction, the cycle of OCD continues in solitude and isolation because it is often simply not talked about. Even in therapy, it never occurred to me to talk about plucking out my eyelashes and eyebrows, not even with the one person in my world who might have understood. Not once did I bring it up; not once did it *occur* to me bring it up, the shame was so deep and ingrained. Fortunately, over the years, addiction has gotten more and more screen time and does not carry quite the cloak of shame it once did. You won't necessarily find many of us in recovery shouting it from the rooftops, but then again there are even support groups in many high schools these days. Hopefully, OCD will one day find a similar degree of understanding among the general population because that acceptance and dialogue are what we need, not necessarily to break the cycle of repetitive behavior, since sometimes we can and sometimes we can't, but to break the cycle of shame. Because I can tell you from experience, the shame is a killer.

CHAPTER TWO
YELLOW BELT

"YELLOW IS THE SYMBOL OF THE FIRST RAYS OF THE SUN SHINING ON THE SEED. YELLOW CAN ALSO SYMBOLIZE THE EARTH, IN WHICH THE SEED SENDS ITS ROOTS FOR NOURISHMENT. A STUDENT EARNS A YELLOW SASH BY ALLOWING HIS MIND TO BE OPENED TO THE KNOWLEDGE OF HIS INSTRUCTORS."

~GWEN BRUNO, LIVESTRONG.COM

Sarcasm is a big part of my life; it was for many years a main line of defense against people who might hurt me. I've managed it over the years so that, for example, I try not to use it against my kids, but it still pops up from time to time if someone says something I consider particularly stupid.

One of the few times I was ever scolded—in my entire life, actually, because I was a rule-follower—was in karate one night when I was a lower belt and hadn't yet quite learned all the rules. Or learned to control my sarcasm, for that matter. The instructor—a child, as far as I could tell, and probably eighteen years old to my thirty—was a stern, no-nonsense young man who seemed to enjoy his role as master over us a little too thoroughly. I quietly shared my suspicion with my warm-up partner, but not quietly enough; the instructor came over and said, "I don't want to hear your voice again today."

He didn't hear it for weeks, if I recall correctly. But he remains in my memory as the first person brave enough to tell me to listen instead of talk.

1970, AGE EIGHT.

The cat had kittens—four of them.

"We each get one!" my little brother gleefully suggests. He's five, so I'm guessing he has no idea that there's no way our mom will let us each have one of the neighbor's kittens, or even one for the family, for that matter. I'm also guessing he has no idea what goes into caring for a pet. I know better. I know we have to feed them and make sure they have water and play with them and soothe them. I know we have to hold them and pet them and show them they're loved. We have to protect them and make sure they don't get hurt or stuck in a tree or run over by a horse. At eight, I know what makes a good parent.

Nevertheless, we all pretend we can choose one for our own. Third in line, I get to pick from the last two kittens: a gray one and a black one. I know my little brother has his heart set on the black one, so I take the gray one. He barely fills the palm of my hand, he's so small. Even in our fantasy, we can't have them yet because they're only a few days old, so we give them back to the momma cat to feed. She lives in the barn and has made a nice little bed for them in the hay. I watch how she tends them, how gentle she is as she cleans them with her tongue. The thought of hair in my mouth makes me gag, so I don't think too much about that part.

We return to the barn every few hours or so to visit our new pets, to make sure they recognize us and love us and want to be with us and follow us around and sleep with us, convinced that my mother will ultimately see the logic in letting each of us keep one. After all, the boy across the road has two black labs, Maudie and Bandit, who watch over him. They sleep with him and follow him around his house and swim with him in his pond, and he's probably never lonely. That's what pets are for, and how could she not want that for us? It would be my first real pet, if you don't count the snapping turtles my older brother finds in the pond and relocates to the old bathtub in the pasture, which I don't.

After a few days, the kittens' eyes are open and they're seeing us and mewing and crawling all over each other and their mother. We pick up our charges and take them to separate spots in the yard to get to know them, and to give them a chance to get to know us. I love my little guy so much it hurts. I don't want to give him back to the mother, but I know I have to. He has to eat.

I make his bed: a box with an old towel in it to make it soft and cozy. I glue a little broken mirror to the inside of the box because he might like to look at himself. I head out to the barn to present his new "home" for inspection, but the kittens aren't there.

The mother cat is hiding under a tractor wheel. I can see her. I hear mewing all over the place and follow my ears to three confused, scared kittens scattered among the hay bales. I pick them all up and put them back in their momma's bed, and start to look for the fourth kitten—the gray one. Mine.

He is nowhere to be found in the barn. I step outside into the glaring sunlight and catch a glimpse of the dogs. Maudie's sniffing along the ground by a bush. As I walk toward her, Bandit comes trotting around the corner of the barn carrying something in his mouth. I freeze for a moment, and then run at him screaming, "Drop it! Drop it!" Surprised by the sound of my voice, he does.

I gently pick it up and stroke its limp neck, and suddenly I'm sobbing. I run back to the house, cradling my kitten in my cupped hands, crying, "Bandit killed my kitten!" My heart is broken like my little kitten's neck, and I want to curl up in his little bed and die with him.

I HAVE FIVE SIBLINGS, TWO OF WHOM WERE BORN MUCH LATER THAN THE REST OF US.

Of the four older kids, there are three boys and me. As with siblings all over the world from the beginning of time, we were alternately each other's best friends, protectors, and tormentors, moving from reading together to beating each other in the space of minutes. We also perfected, as did siblings all over the world from the beginning of time, the dreaded art of indifference, because if you don't care, then it doesn't hurt. In fact, it's tough to say where more of my energy went during those years: trying to make them love me or trying not to care when they didn't.

The place we spent most of our childhood was that farm we rented. In addition to the basic farm animals, there was an enormous pasture that encompassed about fifty acres of land and contained two ponds.

The pasture also housed the fabled manure pile next to the barn.

We would play in that pile of shit until we couldn't take the bugs anymore, and then we'd find something else to do in the pasture: look for polliwogs or turtles or snakes; climb the hay baler up to the hayloft and play hide-and-seek; look for treasures in the big, old shed that housed farm equipment held together by rust. And while I know this can't possibly be true because we only had one car and my dad had it all the time, it seemed like we were going to the emergency room for tetanus shots with frightening regularity.

The horses on the farm ranged from an ancient, fat pony named Pat to dizzyingly tall, sleek, boarded race horses, none of which belonged to us. We rode them sometimes and tried to stay out of their way most times—not always an easy task since our playground was essentially their home.

The pond where we spent much of our time was inconveniently located in the horse pasture, so we had to invade their territory to reach it. It was a great pond. In the winter, we'd lace up our skates and head down to the pond with our shovels, hoping to God it stayed frozen once we got on the ice. Once we shoveled off the snow, we'd skate until we couldn't feel our feet and then trek back up to the house. I can still recall the sensation of warmth and the pain as the feeling returning to my toes. Once we got warmed up, we'd put plastic bread bags on our feet so our boots would slide on, suit-up in our snowmobile suits and boots, and head back out to play.

In the summer, it was a different world down there. The pond had a little stream leading into it, which gave us endless hours of polliwog pleasure, and there were just enough snapping turtles to add an element of danger that makes swimming so much fun for kids. We could spend hours searching for wildlife in that little strip of water: salamanders, frogs, snakes. We were little croc hunters back then—fearless.

The pond was also our tropical paradise on the hot days of summer. We were all swimmers at a young age, and, while I never lost my fear of snapping turtles, I actually got used to removing the leeches that would find our legs as we sunk into the muddy bottom of the edge of the water. The horses, over time, had beaten a path from the pasture around the pond and back to the barn, and that last part of the path was the one we used as well. One day we were swimming with our cousins while the horses grazed in the field. When we were finished, we headed back on the path. We were halfway to the barn when we heard galloping horse hooves, looked back, and realized the horses were stampeding toward us.

My brothers and cousins broke right and jumped back in the pond. I somehow thought I'd be safer if I made for the fence, twice the distance of the pond, and broke left. After two steps, I tripped and fell on my stomach, and that's where my brothers and cousins found me after all of the horses had run over me.

Amazingly, I was only badly bruised, establishing an unnerving trend in my life of not getting seriously hurt, even when I technically should have been. Nothing was broken, including my back, although I gave my mother a good scare when she saw me approaching the house being carried home like a broken doll over my brother's shoulder. I still have dreams about running toward that fence. Sometimes in my dreams, I make it.

There were other horse incidents over the years: my little brother being bucked over the head of a mammoth racehorse on which he was being led; an older brother and a neighbor racing from one end of a field to another and the brother's horse returning *sans* saddle and rider; my favorite pony, Pat, taking off into some trees with me on his back, losing my glasses and much skin to an unyielding branch as he dashed under it.

None of those compared to what happened when I was ten, when Pat got out of the pasture in the middle of the night and stood there in the dark, in the middle of the road. That's where we found him the next morning, right in front of the VW that was totaled when it hit him. He was lying on his side, his stomach split open, intestines spilling out, and the neighbor boy had to move him to the side of the road.

By that time, I'd already lost a grandfather, but nothing hurt like losing that horse and that kitten. Even today, the loss of an animal evokes a visceral reaction: a pain so deep it threatens to slice me in two. It hurts me to lose loved ones, but it darn near kills me to lose animals.

MY BLESSING—OR CURSE—IS MY ABILITY TO GLORIFY MY PAST.

In my mind, my childhood was a series of exciting adventures shared with my brothers on this rented farm with horses and ponds. In my mind, we enjoyed cutting down our Christmas tree each year from across the road and watching thunderstorms from the shed; picking wild strawberries in the field and playing hide-and-seek in the tall grass. However, I know the reality was different.

I know my dad was an alcoholic, even though the word was never spoken.

We lived in a culture of secrecy back then. Celebrities weren't coming out of the closet yet or admitting to being addicts or suffering from depression. The government was tap-dancing around the Vietnam conflict and a president was impeached over secret wire-tapping. No one talked about their parents getting divorced or beating them or sexually abusing them. Drug abuse was hushed up, suicide was hushed up, unwed mothers were hushed up. Sexually transmitted diseases were still a taboo subject, as was birth control to a great extent. Secrets were the order of the day.

So keeping our own family secret wasn't a big reach.

It was, however, a heavy burden. My dad had lived a challenging life, and the leftover anger that was usually under control became less so when he drank. It seemed as though I moved through life in a haze of fear, guilt, embarrassment, and shame. Fear because I never knew what to expect at home. Guilt over whatever it was I did that made my dad angry, and even more over secretly wishing sometimes, under the covers in the dark, that he just wouldn't come home—and then panicking when he was later than usual because if something happened to him it would be my fault. Embarrassment because I couldn't have friends over like other kids could. And shame because that's what's left when fear, guilt, and embarrassment are kept secret. It's released in the sharing of it, the acknowledgment—the confession. If that confession never comes, then those other qualities become permanent fixtures in the brain.

It wasn't so bad while we were living it because, for some of the time at least, we didn't know any different. How do you know, if you've experienced no other life, that anybody else's life is better than yours? Ah, but therein lay the double-edged sword; when you have nothing to compare the bad to, it's not so bad because maybe everyone else has the same kind of life. When you finally do have something to compare it to—a friend's "normal" life, for instance—it's as bad as it can possibly be. You could have certainly colored me surprised when I realized I shared that disease of addiction with my father; there really weren't enough apologies in the world—from either of us, probably—that could make us feel better for how we treated each other. He had to get over the way his disease impacted our childhoods; I had to get over my anger at him for it, and combine that release with my newfound knowledge that it's a really, really hard thing to break free from.

Except for the occasional scabs, there were only one or two other rituals that permeated my daily life. I sucked my thumb until I was seven, and, when I lost my favorite blanket with the silky edges, I found the fatty tissue on the inside of my thigh to be just as comforting. I'd lie in bed with my thumb in my mouth and fondle that fatty tissue until I fell asleep. If the scab-picking was the first thing I was too ashamed to tell my mom, then the inner-thigh-fondling was the second.

I wasn't self-mutilating yet, although my OCD manifestations had begun: the hamster wheel of anxiety, followed by whatever ritual was primary at the time—counting, plucking, picking—a ritual I did not want to perform but was unable to stop, which caused more anxiety. I was eventually able to kick the thumb-sucking habit with the help of some public humiliation by others and a strategically placed Band-Aid or two, cementing in the process—for future reference—the value of secrecy. And I did know this: Turning my anger and insecurity inward actually provided some release.

MY MOTHER WAS MY HERO IN THOSE EARLY YEARS.

She represented—still represents—all that was right with the world, and any insidious doubts I had as to why she defended my father were pushed way down deep for later. She was perfect: She was kind and gentle and loving and giving and smart. I adored and idolized her. If I did something wrong, which was rare, I could not function again until she had forgiven me—which I later found out is another manifestation of OCD.

I obsessively cleaned the house for her, particularly when she was out shopping so that she would be surprised upon her return. I lived for those moments when she walked through the door and found a clean house. I was the best then; I was her perfect little girl, in the middle of those not-so-perfect boys. My secrets were safe, they were not adversely affecting people's perceptions of me, and the anxiety was held at bay by that perfection. I was the princess. I used to lie to the priest in confession because I didn't have any sins to confess, the irony of which made for much amusement later in life.

One day, my mother came into the bathroom and found me crying in front of the mirror. She came up behind me, pulled my wet, stringy hair out of my face, and said, "Aw, honey . . . I tried so hard to make you like yourself. I always tell you how beautiful you are, and smart, and what a good girl, and how much I love you, because I never liked myself and I know how hard it is. Please like yourself, honey. I don't know what else to do for you."

I was touched by her confession for a moment, felt a fleeting camaraderie even, and then a kind of devastation started to sink in.

If she didn't like herself either, then how could I ever like myself?

You can't give someone what you haven't got, plain and simple. My mom couldn't possibly have given me self-confidence and self-esteem because she didn't have them to give. Although I tried to hide my disappointment, the illusion of perfection was shattered—of my mom's and my own. I was crushed, and subtly our relationship changed. Maybe that's what the teen years do to a mother-daughter relationship, anyway: the pulling away, the "Okay, fine; if you're not going to help me, I'll do it myself" method of independence.

As I grew older, more mature and somewhat more knowledgeable about the goings-on in the family, my relationship with my mother shifted yet again and I found myself trying to save her, to protect her, and to make her stand up for herself. How amusing she must have thought me at the time: "Here, Mom, let me show you how to do it!" But she never dismissed me. She kept doing what she needed to do to give my youngest siblings the best home she could. It took me years to "forgive" her for being who she is and to forgive myself for blaming her for it.

She was my mother, and she was human, and she was doing the best job she could. She was raising six kids under very trying circumstances. When I realized she was not perfect, I also realized I must not be perfect. It was *me* who disappointed me. As do probably many parents and children, we eventually came full circle, with me growing up and understanding that my mom is one of the strongest women I know, and my mom realizing I had some demons to conquer before being capable of that understanding. On that common ground, over time, we have built a relationship I cherish every day.

Not a day goes by, as I watch my daughter grow up and learn to navigate the world, when I don't hear those words: How can you give something you haven't got?

EVERY YEAR, OUR COUSINS WOULD COME AND VISIT US FOR A WEEK FROM THE MIDWEST.

My uncle was my mom's twin brother, and he and my aunt were two of the happiest people I'd ever known. They had two children: a boy who was my older brother's age and a girl who was a year younger than me.

We would wait for their arrival with great anticipation, sitting on the front steps of the house if it was nice out or huddling just inside the shed if it was raining, screaming and shouting to my mom when we saw their car approaching down the road. The initial hugs, kisses, and backslapping were soon followed by the typical and perpetual competition between my brother and cousin: Who was taller? Stronger? Faster? Normal boy stuff, which we ate up like it was dessert.

The sense of normalcy, however, was eventually clouded by what seemed at the time like two cultures colliding. It was more than just city versus country. It was the realization, with each passing year, that my cousins had a completely different reality than I did. It's as though, in them, I finally had something to compare my situation to. And the comparison kind of hurt.

It probably wasn't even just their wealth, in retrospect. That only explained the material differences. When I was with my female cousin, I was more in awe of her complete normalcy, her ability to say what was on her mind, to talk to her mother and father with the same ease that she talked to us or her brother. She seemed to have no secrets, nothing to hide—from me or from her parents. She was just a typical, well-adjusted girl, and I spent each annual week with her trying to decipher how she did it. When I couldn't, I was frustrated—frustrated and jealous.

It was as simple as that. They had become my benchmark of what a childhood could be, and mine did not measure up. I was jealous of my cousins' lives, of their family, of their wealth, of the fact that they only had two kids. I was jealous that their parents seemed genuinely happy and the kids genuinely liked each other and their parents. They had nice clothes and they took vacations and were rarely, if ever, mean to each other. We played the newest records when they visited, laughing and dancing together. My uncle and I did "the bump" to Captain & Tennille's "Love Will Keep Us Together."

They couldn't have been more normal, or more perfect. And we couldn't have been sadder when they left, or more relieved.

THE "EYELASH ISSUE" WAS WHAT I LIKED TO CALL IT.
Back then, I didn't know there was a word for it: trichotillomania. It first appeared in third grade, or at least was exposed in third grade. I was sitting next to a friend on the bus on the way to school. She was talking about something and suddenly stopped and stared at me. "Where are your eyelashes?" she asked. "There's a whole clump missing!"

She thought it was funny, and I was mortified—not that I'd plucked out a clump of eyelashes, but that I'd gotten caught. I knew then that discretion would be a must. I would learn as time went on not to pluck in clumps, in an effort to camouflage the end result.

There are two incidents in elementary school that stand out in my mind, and that was one of them. The other was, in its own way, equally disturbing.

Out of all of the students, we lived the farthest away from school, and so we were the last off the bus in the afternoon. Midway home, I heard some boys in the back of the bus making fun of me for some reason or other, and suddenly I felt something hit the back of my head. My hand flew to my hair and came back with the longest string of snot I'd ever seen. I was horrified, disgusted, revolted, and silent. I acted like nothing had happened. Because the most important life lesson I'd learned by then was never to show humiliation.

What I didn't know then, but believe now, is that this is part of the cycle of OCD: the shame, guilt, and self-hatred that I'd already been feeling. When a child, or even an adult, experiences obsessive thoughts and/or rituals and believes no one else experiences them, he keeps them to himself. He suffers silently, struggles silently, fights it, and fails silently. The effects of that ongoing cycle of shame on his self-esteem can be catastrophic and long-term.

It's a vicious circle: I have obsessive thoughts and uncontrollable urges that seemingly no one else has, which cause my self-esteem to plummet; since I have such a low opinion of myself, I feel I don't deserve to be with other people, to love other people, or to let other people love me; the loneliness and self-hatred cause anxiety, which kicks the OCD into high gear, compelling me to do things to myself that will further my isolation because I make myself ugly by scarring my face or plucking out my hair.

Sometimes I wonder if picking at my face to get the zits off, for example, is a metaphor for how I would like my life to be: smooth, flawless. The same could be said of the TTM; the end result of plucked eyebrows and eyelashes is perfectly smooth skin. Too easy an assumption? Maybe. There's also the train of thought that suggests I mutilate my face to be more unattractive because I inherently believe I don't deserve to be pretty. Could people like me keep psychiatrists busy? Oh, yes.

There's another part of the OCD process, though, one that's at once easy and indescribably difficult to understand, and it is this:

When I'm plucking, or picking at my face, or stepping on and off that scale, or counting, the world is on hold. I'm completely away. My brain shuts down and I'm focused on my task. It's as though I'm able to shut myself off from life entirely for those few minutes. I escape. And nothing hurts.

In fact, it's almost like meditation—a distorted, perverse, self-destructive meditation technique. Maybe I could develop an OCD mantra and market it to the masses.

I've tried, many times, cutting my fingernails as short as they can go without bleeding because, of course, fingernails are a key component of both the picking and plucking process; you can't pick and pluck what you can't grasp, right? And that actually works for a while, until the nails start to grow back and I can't control myself because, while my face may be okay, now my lashes and brows have been growing for, what, weeks? And they *need to be smooth.*

And then there's the pain: the absolutely exquisite pain of pulling out the deepest part of a pimple—the root—from under the skin. There's something to that, I'm sure; getting to the root of the problem, perhaps? Because it's the same thing with my eyelashes. In fact, that's what it's all about. Pulling lashes out by the root has a completely different physical effect than, for instance, trimming them with scissors. It hurts. So it's not that I want to have no eyelashes or eyebrows; it's that I want to pull them out. That's where the pain is, and, therefore, the satisfaction.

In recalling the Band-Aid solution to the thumb-sucking problem, it would seem that, despite the rudimentary solutions, I've always been pretty adept at seeing there's a problem, so that's helpful. They say that knowing there's a problem is half the solution, but here's the flaw in that thinking when it comes to people like me: The other half of the solution involves telling someone, which we cannot do.

ANOREXIA WAS A LITTLE EASIER TO GET AWAY WITH IN THE OLD DAYS.

Both the word and the concept were at least as foreign as OCD to most people. When I was in fifth grade, my mother got pregnant with her fifth child. My youngest brother was only eight and my two older brothers were, well, boys, and back then nothing was expected of any of them but taking out the garbage and cutting the grass. I became chief bottle-washer, diaper-changer, and middle-of-the-night nanny for my new sibling, whom I loved dearly.

But loving him was apparently not enough for me to get past the upheaval. He shared my bedroom, and he was not a particularly good sleeper. He could cry—scream—for hours, and the philosophy back then was to let babies cry it out, whether or not their older sister is sleeping in the same room, eyes glued to the clock, with a knot in her stomach because she has to get up for school at 6:00 a.m.

That year we had our annual school physical. We would walk down to the nurse's office as a class and wait our turn to get weighed and measured; it was something to look forward to every year because we all wanted to get taller. This time, however, my best friend came out of that nurse's office weighing four pounds less than me, and I lost a little part of my mind.

This was before Karen Carpenter, before anorexia nervosa was presented as a legitimate mental condition, before movie stars and famous people exposed their personal battles in the pages of *People* magazine. The TV shows we watched were *All in the Family* and *The Brady Bunch* and *Night Stalker*. There were no music videos, no Calvin Klein underwear ads, no 24/7 Internet exposure to sickly thin models and celebrities. This was 1972 and I was a ten-year-old girl who decided she was fat simply because she weighed more than her best friend.

I started on an obsessive game plan of losing weight as discreetly as possible. Sometimes I would be able to starve for days at a time without anyone noticing; other times I would binge and correct. For instance, one time, when my mother had brought home a special treat of candy bars for each of us, I ate mine and then went outside and ran around the house thirty times. My oldest brother watched me curiously, and when I came in he asked, "Wouldn't it have been easier to just not eat the candy bar?"

Since dubbed "the candy bar incident," it was the first in a long line of classic distortions between what is and what should be. But I did manage to lose weight. My mom's best friend was visiting her one day, and I'd just received a box of hand-me-downs from the older girl across the road. I modeled my new-old clothes for them, and later that day my mom said, "Donna thinks I'm being too lax with your eating." But that was it. My mom got pregnant again and had my sister the following summer. The good news— for me, anyway—was that I dropped ten pounds from fifth grade to sixth. The bad news—again, for me—was that it didn't seem important to anyone else.

CHAPTER THREE

ORANGE BELT

> "ORANGE IS THE SYMBOL OF THE INCREASING POWER OF THE SUN AS IT WARMS THE EARTH AND MAKES PLANTS GROW. THE ORANGE-BELT STUDENT BEGINS TO DEVELOP BOTH PHYSICALLY AND MENTALLY IN HIS MARTIAL ARTS DISCIPLINE."
>
> ~GWEN BRUNO, LIVESTRONG.COM

By orange belt, I'd befriended three other women around my age; we had all begun classes at about the same time and we naturally fell together. I was much more comfortable having a "crew," as it were; we were learning *katas* and *kumites* and self-defense techniques that were easier to master with a friendly face standing by.

We'd also learned just enough material to be cocky about our training. By then I was comfortable going with my friends and not drinking, and we would hang out in bars on weekends, doing our self-defense moves on each other and putting our *katas* to the dance music. We all had key chains reflecting our current belt levels. We were not yet great practitioners of the modesty aspect of the Student Creed.

1975, AGE THIRTEEN.

I wake up this morning with butterflies in my stomach. Our sixth-grade class is going roller-skating, and the first crush of my middle school years will be there. We've made a lot of eye contact over the past few days, and I'm gearing up to say "hello" at the roller rink. I've spent an embarrassing amount of time daydreaming about this boy, and if he merely glances at me while passing in the halls, I'm high for days. Not only has he been glancing at me, we've actually stared at each other. Nothing can bring me down. Life is good. I've been looking forward to this roller skating party more than anything I've ever looked forward to in my life.

I come downstairs with my baby brother and notice that absolutely nobody is speaking, although everyone is up. The kitchen is quiet, devoid of the usual AM radio station that is my mother's constant morning companion. As I pass the bathroom, I notice that my father's not doing his shaving thing, as is the norm when I get up. I think, Jeez, this is the first time I can remember that I can actually go to the bathroom as soon as I get up, and I don't have to go! I smile at the irony and carry the baby into the kitchen. My brothers are just sitting at the table, staring at their cereal. My mom's leaning against the counter crying, and my dad's standing at the opposite counter watching her.

My mom takes the baby from me and uses the break in the tension to clear her throat and get herself together. She tells me what has happened. A cousin who was several years older than me, and who had recently returned from Viet Nam, was killed in a motorcycle accident last night. He "failed to negotiate a curve" while on his way home from the bar where his brother, my godfather, worked. My godfather left the bar a few minutes later and found him on the road.

They must have just gotten the phone call, based on the dazed looks on all of their faces. My mom begins crying again as she relates what my aunt had told her, and I take the baby back, get his bottle, and sit on the couch in the living room to feed him. As I sit there, I feel the familiar pang of disappointment snake its way through my stomach. I realize that the roller skating party will not happen for me, and when I finally get up the nerve to voice that concern to my mother, she looks at me as though I have two heads. She doesn't understand.

It's not that I'm not sad about my cousin dying. I am. I'm sorry for him and for my godfather and for my aunt and uncle and their other children, my cousins. I'm sorry for my mom and dad and all of our other relatives who will mourn his loss. It's just that bad things always happen in our family. Roller skating parties don't.

MIDDLE SCHOOL WAS THE LEARNING EXPERIENCE FOR ME THAT IT WAS FOR MOST GIRLS.

We were all concerned about who would get their period first and whether the girls who already had their period were going to get breasts first and, therefore, get boyfriends first. There was a lot of competition back then, all based, as far as I could tell, on looks and clothes and little purses with wooden handles and clogs and monogrammed sweaters. If you had all that stuff, you were "in," and if you didn't, you weren't. I didn't have any of that stuff. After much nagging and begging and pleading, my mom bought me a pair of clogs, but they were rubber Kmart clogs and not the good kind with the leather upper and wooden heel. I finally became "cool" at age fifty when I realized I could afford the real thing and ordered them online. Better late than never.

It was also during this period of my life that my fear of people being mad spread from my family to my friends. I felt a perpetual sense of blame; I would say "I'm sorry" the way other people say "the." I apologized for everything, whether it was my fault or not. I was sorry if it was raining, sorry if a friend got a bad grade on a test, sorry if my little brother or sister wouldn't stop crying. Finally, my friends started telling me to stop saying it, and I'd then say I was sorry for saying "I'm sorry." I had to constantly choose what was less debilitating—the need to apologize, or the need to not have people mad at me.

It was a black period, I recall, because I really did feel that every single thing was somehow my fault. It took months and months of deliberate practice and friends' help to stop saying it, and another several years of living to stop feeling it. In my OCD world, that was probably when my fear of people being mad was kicking in full-time; the apologizing was an almost pathological attempt to ward off that compulsive feeling. It was the beginning of the trend in my life to consciously, and then unconsciously, avoid any and all situations that could result in my disappointing or angering someone. Even today when wronged—blatantly disrespected, abused even—I simply cannot say the words that need to be said for fear of making someone angry.

I wonder sometimes if that part of my OCD was also what drove my need to achieve; if I got a bad grade, would the teacher be mad? Would my mom be disappointed? I grew up with a complete inability to handle confrontation or difficult conversations—even the composed, civilized kind—and so I learned to go out of my way to avoid them. This often meant learning to live with situations that were unhealthy and sometimes downright dangerous, and it's one of my bigger regrets. You have to be able to speak up for yourself. It should be the eleventh commandment.

Around that same time was when I began to sweat in earnest and discovered a new, completely unanticipated embarrassment. Regular deodorant was not very effective for me, a fact that came as a complete shock, particularly when I spent the majority of my waking hours trying to go unnoticed. I was more prepared for my period than I was for sweat. One day in school, I realized that my armpits were soaked, and I fled to the bathroom where I splashed water all over the front and back and sides of my shirt in the hopes that anyone who noticed would think that the sweat was simply a result of an unfortunate hand-washing accident.

BACK THEN WAS PROBABLY WHEN WE ALL LEARNED OUR LITTLE SURVIVAL TRICKS.

Those of us who did learn them, that is. My oldest brother was an athlete, excelling at multiple sports. As the firstborn, he was responsible and always mature for his years. He did well academically and played guitar and was always busy; I was always slightly in awe of him. My next older brother, who I always likened with some admiration to a volcano perpetually on the verge of eruption, learned at a young age how to hunt and trap, and during the season he would often be gone from dawn until dusk. When he got home, he'd go down to the basement to skin his catch until it was bedtime.

Occasionally, he would let me hang out with him in the basement while he skinned his animals. Fox, mink, muskrat, possum— whatever he caught in his traps he skinned and sold. Although I was not interested in skinning anything, I'd go down there for the sheer thrill of being allowed. It was a cellar like all old cellars, with stone walls and a dank smell that was made worse by the activities that went on down there. At any given time, there were a dozen pelts nailed to boards in varying stages of drying and stinking. We also had a Ping-Pong table down there, at which we would play until someone got mad and walked out. Or, come to think of it, until the smell overcame us.

From time to time, we would target-shoot with BB rifles down in that basement, the little round metal balls careening off the stone walls if they failed to embed in the paper target. Those were our bonding times, few and far between. And, almost impossibly, no one ever put their eye out.

My younger brother was my Godsend. He was cute and sweet and never, ever doubted that I was the best big sister a guy could have. We sang and danced to the records that my mom often played on the console stereo, we peeled the skin off of each other's sunburned backs, had foot wars on the couch while watching television, and generally gave each other the kind of emotional support that only the luckiest siblings get to experience. He was my sanity when I was young, proof beyond the obligatory behavior of parents that I was capable of being loved.

My youngest brother and sister grew up in a different situation from the rest of us because the family moved out of the country and into the village when they were babies. They didn't play in the manure pile and swim in the pond and walk past a half-skinned muskrat to get to the kitchen. They didn't wander unattended from dawn until dusk or play with BB guns in the basement or ride horses in the corral or play on a hook in the hay loft.

They did, however, have four older siblings to look up to and a nice little town at their disposal. The bad news for them was that because we were now in the village, we older siblings were never home anymore. We didn't have to be, and we didn't want to be. So, although the move was a fabulous turn of events for us older kids, as far as the younger ones were concerned, we were visitors in their lives who, without exception, eventually left them.

My own coping mechanism was simple: Do whatever it takes to seem normal. In my memory, I never complained, never cried, never talked back to my parents, never instigated fights with my brothers. I was mature, responsible, intelligent, fair, and very, very Catholic. I never expressed to my mother that I was sad, nervous, scared, or angry. It simply wasn't her problem. She had enough to worry about. And there was always, always, the obsessive fear of making her mad, not because she'd do anything to me—because she wouldn't—but because I simply couldn't function if I thought I had let her down.

From that magical ability to appear normal sprang another handy tool: being able to mask or completely hide my mental issues. I managed my obsessive thoughts the best I could, learning to function around them, and the same happened with the rituals. Many of them were in my head—the counting, for example— and the rest, which came and went and shifted form, I managed to incorporate fairly seamlessly into my life. But I could always tell when things were going to get worse. It takes a lot of energy to seem happy, you know; there's a lot of stress involved. A girl has to have outlets for that stress, and given enough time and enough stress, she'll find some. Or some will find her.

MY PARENTS HAD THEIR OWN WAYS OF COPING BACK THEN.

It was handed down to them from their parents and their parents' parents. Drinking was the way it was done throughout their history, and they followed in the only footsteps they knew: My dad drank, and my mom married a drinker. They both had much to overcome from their own childhoods in a generation where such overcoming was unheard of. There was little therapy and even less sympathy. If there was a generational motto, it would have been, "Suck it up."

My dad was a yeller, and his yelling voice sent shivers down my spine. He was not a violent man, though, and aside from his generation's typical belief in occasional corporal punishment being good for the soul, most of his punishment was doled out verbally. We were probably the first kids on the proverbial block to take exception to the old "sticks and stones" adage, though; we knew words could maim.

There were times when we would have preferred a whip. It was as if he knew our deepest, darkest insecurities, and that's where he'd aim, with the sarcasm that, in our adult years, we'd try to best. Of course, now I know how he knew all those deep, dark insecurities; it couldn't have been more obvious, like the pile of manure. He knew them because they were all his insecurities as well.

My dad was a very smart man who was dealt a crappy hand, and he did the best with what he had. We were never homeless and we were never hungry. And he was probably never happy, at least not until he quit drinking. I'm hoping he's been happy since then because he deserves it. But if anyone knows, I do; being sober, while awesome, does not necessarily assuage the guilt and damage of the past.

It seemed back then, particularly in high school, that we were always waiting for him to get home with the car so we could go someplace—a basketball game, football game, baseball game— always waiting, watching the clock. I finally learned how to convince myself, until I truly believed it, that it was okay, that I didn't really want to go, anyway. I learned, eventually and for the rest of my life, not to get my hopes up about anything, not to expect a lot. Low expectations mean little disappointment.

And then, inexplicably, I'd see him every Sunday as a different person. He'd sit in his rocking chair—no television, no music— and just sit and rock and stare off into space, and I knew he was thinking about stuff that I knew nothing about. And I realized as I got older, little by little and week after week, that he was hurting and trying to deal with it the best he could.

He was human to me on those Sundays—human and vulnerable and sad. My dad's father was an alcoholic, his mother died when he was young, and he was sent to live with relatives, many of whom were also alcoholic. He probably felt—and I'm guessing here because I've never asked and I'm not sure he even knows— that he wasn't providing for his family well enough, fueling a sense of failure, fueling his drinking.

He'd had a really tough time of it growing up, and then as soon as he was out of school, *bam!*—he now had a wife and four kids and a job at a truck stop in an industry with limited options for advancement. He also had a sixty-hour work week because of us, his kids—his kids who couldn't, wouldn't, even hold a conversation with him at the dinner table that involved more than one-word answers.

And that's what I knew of my dad back then: that he was a smart man who had many reasons to be angry at the alcoholic gene of generations before him. Sober now longer than me, it turns out that without the alcohol, he's an awesome person. But the shame that shrouded this disease in those days was crippling, for him and for us. It's not an excuse for what happened to me, though, and I'm not even sure it's an explanation; it is what it is. I know there are millions of kids who grow up worse off than I did who don't do the things I've done to myself.

ONE OF MY DAD'S PASSIONS WAS MUSIC.

If he got home late, he would inevitably head for the living room; that's where his real emotional safety net awaited in the form of a record player.

He loved his music. Unfortunately, he loved it really loud, and would often blast it into the night. The Rolling Stones, Johnny Cash, Kris Kristofferson, The Beatles: those were the biggies.

Those are the ones I couldn't listen to for years as an adult without breaking down into tears.

Yet I do listen now. I took all those albums with me one time when I was home because I wanted to remember—needed to remember—more about my life, and I knew those songs would bring some of it back. After all of those years of pushing my pillow against my ears to block out the music, trying desperately to hold it when I had to go to the bathroom because I had to walk right past the living room to get there—after all of that, I now needed it to reclaim my life. As the title of an album by the Rolling Stones, one of my dad's all-time favorites, said, sometimes you must go "through the past, darkly."

Ironically, music became our savior. My oldest brother played guitar, the second oldest played drums, the younger played keyboards, and I played a little piano and a mean tambourine. There was an older boy across the road who played bass, and when we were younger we would all jam up in our attic bedroom—as much as you can jam at four, seven, eight, and ten years old. We were the Partridge Family, without the wacky adventures.

My brothers went on to be gifted musicians. I was an average piano player and instead found my "gift" in lyrics. I didn't write them, but I was able, without even trying, to memorize every word of every song I ever heard. I can name that tune in three drumbeats, sometimes one note, and am a relentless trivia player when it comes to seventies music. Yes, only seventies. I don't know why, except that the seventies produced the single best decade-worth of music in history. I'm pretty sure that's a fact somewhere. You can look it up.

There is at least one song per phase of life, even toddlerhood, that can reduce me to tears and my muscles to Jell-O. I danced with my little brother to "Winchester Cathedral" and "Cecilia." I plotted my escape from my home life in the wee hours of the morning to my father's blaring "Paint It Black" and "I Walk the Line." I cried with my oldest brother because we thought "Puff the Magic Dragon" died.

My grammar school memories are linked to "Tie a Yellow Ribbon Round the Ole Oak Tree" and "Knock Three Times"; in fact, singer Tony Orlando may well have been my first crush. Those songs bring back the smell of paste and construction paper and the sense of walking through the halls of elementary school as though on eggshells, obsessed even then with trying to fit in and seem like the other kids. I was too young to identify what was wrong with me, and too old to pretend the feeling wasn't there.

Then there was "Nice to Be with You" and "Green-Eyed Lady" and "Sweet City Woman," songs that return me to the field on the farm and playing hide-and-seek in the tall grass because all you had to do was sit down in it and you were invisible. Those songs for some reason gave me hope that there was more to life than what I had.

Next was "Island Girl" and "Tush" and "Spill the Wine" and "Love Will Keep Us Together" and, of course, my first 45 record, "I Think I Love You" by the Partridge Family with the great David Cassidy and his feathered hair. Reality had set in by then and music had truly become an escape. When I listened to it, I could dream, I could imagine, I could pretend I was normal and was going to have a normal life. I could pretend I would be loved.

Middle school gave the world "Mandy" and "I Write the Songs," and "Smoke on the Water" and "Sorry Seems to Be the Hardest Word." We sang *Godspell* in chorus and "The Sound of Silence" and "Take Me Home, Country Roads," for which I was the fifth-grade piano accompanist—a feat that to this day amazes me, given my social anxiety.

And high school? A veritable landscape of memory-strewn music: "Dancing Queen" and "Time for Me to Fly" and "Rock'n Me" and "Stairway to Heaven" and "Free Bird" and anything by Bob Seger and Steely Dan and Peter Frampton. I practiced dancing before a mirror in my Danskin skirt and leotard that I bought with my babysitting money. Music was my fantasy of a better life. Every song was associated with someone new, some significant almost-love in my life; I was always searching, reaching, for that one thing that would make everything okay.

At the time, I had no idea what that music would do to me in later years; it was as if I'd honed this incredible skill of cataloging all of my memories and associated feelings by song title and then filing them and locking them up. I was simply able to forget my past, forget the pain, close it down, put it away. It worked for many years, those years when sixties and seventies music wasn't so easy to come by. Music was my emotional safe deposit box into which I deposited my childhood.

Unfortunately, certain songs unlocked it. When a song came on that had a particular memory connected with it, that memory was temporarily released. When that key turned in the lock, there was nothing I could do except go back—back to that time I was trying so hard to forget. And it wasn't just the memories that came back, it *all* came back: the feelings, the physical ache, the fear, the anger, and the sense that I was worth less than a bug under someone's shoe. Fortunately, once the song was over, the memory, too, was gone, cataloged and locked up once again until the next time it played on the radio.

It was a great system, that box, except for one thing: I didn't control the key.

It would be years before satellite radio came along with its "all seventies, all the time" option, or the iPod, that magical little device that now holds hundreds of those songs from my youth. I listen to them every day, every time I walk my dog, every time I take a long trip. It's my own brand of immersion therapy; I listen to them so that I can remember my past, and then I keep listening until it doesn't hurt anymore. After enough play time, the memories become buffed like sea glass, and the iPod then seems like it's just filled with really great songs from the seventies—or, in some cases, I guess, really bad ones.

CHAPTER FOUR
PURPLE BELT

"PURPLE IS THE SYMBOL OF MOUNTAINS AND THE STEEP PATHS THEY PRESENT. AS THE STUDENT MOVES ON TO HIGHER LEVELS OF ACHIEVEMENT, HE HAS DIFFICULT TASKS TO MASTER. PURPLE CAN ALSO REPRESENT THE SKY AT DAWN, A SYMBOL OF THE CHANGE THAT A STUDENT UNDERGOES AS HE TRANSITIONS TO THE ADVANCED LEVELS OF MARTIAL ARTS."

~GWEN BRUNO, LIVESTRONG.COM

When we became purple belts, we were no longer the newbies, the novices, the uninitiated. There was a whole group of people below us now: beginners learning the basics as we had months earlier. We had settled into a comfortable slot, the group and I;

if all went well, we realized we could possibly get our black belts together. We started hanging out even more and developing a camaraderie that I'd honestly never experienced in my life. I was part of something.

Finally, I belonged.

1977, AGE FIFTEEN.

The homecoming float is being erected in my friend's barn this year, and the sophomore class is going to kick some ass! Woo-hoo! I repeat this to myself as I get ready to go work on the float, as I brush my hair and try to flatten down the frizz and dabble with some of my mom's foundation to maybe cover up a freckle or two. I don't have any cool clothes, and I'm still dying for a pair of those wooden clogs with no dorky straps, but I can't get them.

I call to my mom that I'm leaving for Katie's and head out the door. It's about a ten-minute walk, and it's a beautiful, cool, crisp fall night. I can smell someone's fireplace in the air, and when I'm walking in this atmosphere it's as if nothing in the world is happening around me. I simply am, and I realize how much I missed that feeling since moving into the village this summer.

I walk confidently, as I've taught myself to do, because when I'm alone I can do anything, be anybody. As I come up her driveway, I hear voices—laughing, joking around, mock indignation—and freeze inside. I'm here; I have to go in, but once I go in I'm invisible. I'm not one of those people who go to pep rallies and football games and homecoming dances. My friend is one of those people, but she's been my friend since fifth grade, before these things mattered, and I'm afraid she's kind of stuck with me now.

I enter the barn and take in all that's going on: the flat wagon on which the float is being built; the rolls and rolls of crepe paper being tossed about by the boys who really didn't come here to work; the popular girls up on the float trying to create something out of nothing. I hang back and lean against a wall, wrestling with my ever-present dueling demons of wanting to be seen and wanting to be invisible, and realize that I'm trying to do the same thing as the popular girls are trying to do with the float: create a personality, a life, where there isn't one.

I LOOK AT MY SENIOR PICTURE FROM HIGH SCHOOL.

Each time, I'm again surprised by my clear, smooth skin. And my eyebrows, of course. Any time I see a picture from back then, I am fascinated by my eyebrows—what they used to look like, whether they were even, if they matched my red hair exactly— because now, even when I allow them to grow, however minutely, they're blond. It's as though I don't have them, anyway, which, in turn, helps me justify plucking them out any time I'm anxious. It's your basic vicious circle.

High school opened the floodgates to my self-loathing. The real and imagined anxieties of puberty, combined with the real and imagined anxieties that were already in place, proved to be more than I could handle, and a depression kicked in that would last for years. Any shred of happiness that had managed to survive adolescence disappeared when high school hit.

Fortunately, it was also in high school that I was introduced to the "fake it till you make it" theory of survival. A female friend of my brother's, who was a year ahead of me, was as insecure and self-loathing as I was—that's probably why we connected— but she was funny and so it wasn't as readily apparent that she had "issues." We hung out whenever we could for the simple reason that no explanations were necessary about anything. We understood each other. She took me to a party one night in high school, and I was very nervous.

Before we went in, she took me aside and said, "I have this trick, okay? I use it all the time. You just pretend to be having a good time—really pretend, like you're in a movie and playing a part— and before you know it, you'll really *be* having a good time!" She then went into the party and started mingling and chatting with people and looking to all the world like she belonged.

I tried it for a while but soon realized that my gift was not found in pretending I was having fun. It was pretending I didn't care if I had fun. Pretty soon, faking that came easily.

A poster hung in my bedroom for many years. It started with the words, in huge letters, "I AM ME." It then went on to extol the virtues of being an individual, concluding in equally large print, "I AM OKAY." Sometimes people make me laugh today when they prattle on about the power of self-affirmations, as if they'd discovered them. I was using one forty years ago to keep a gun out of my mouth.

It was also in high school that I discovered the many facets of alcohol. The drinking age then was eighteen, and so most high school graduation parties legally served alcohol, usually in the form of a keg. Since I had two older brothers, I was attending graduation parties in ninth grade.

I loved what alcohol did to me. Long before the concept of self-medicating gained popularity, I knew I loved being drunk. There was a phase of it in which I was happy and confident and everything I wanted to be in real life but wasn't—when nothing was wrong with me or different about me and I was just as cool as the next kid. The hole in my heart that I kept trying to fill with love did not need to be filled when I was loaded. The bad news was that in order to maintain that phase, I had to stop drinking when I reached it, which I never did. Almost without fail I went into the next phase: the angry, crying, throwing-things phase. And even that wasn't so bad as far as I was concerned because I never cried otherwise. It felt good to cry.

I drank every chance I got from tenth grade on. There was a bar conveniently located down the street, which also conveniently served minors, and weekends would find me there shooting pool and hanging out with an older crowd. The bars stayed open until 4:00 a.m., and I figured the later I stayed out, the better the chance my parents would be asleep when I got home—and, of course, the more I could drink.

Somehow, through this bars-open-until-4:00-a.m. behavior, I gained a reputation as a slut in high school, which was so off base as to be laughable. I'm not sure I ever kissed a boy in high school, although it might've happened and just been so shrouded in alcohol as to be unmemorable. Maybe people assumed that since I was out at the bars and shitfaced, I was going home with guys. I wasn't. I stumbled home alone, sometimes crying, sometimes hysterical, but always alone.

My mom used to say that people thought her conceited in high school, misreading her shyness for arrogance; maybe people were misreading my propensity to stay out all night for being easy. I guess it could happen.

Actually, I'd decided long before high school, through careful reading of women's magazines and *Teen Beat*, that the way to be cool was to be aloof, uncaring, untouchable. This would make boys want me. Boys didn't like girls who were needy, clingy, or dependent—all the things I was—and so, in true "fake it till you make it" fashion, I pretended I was totally independent with no need for friends or love. I didn't pay attention to the boys at school or the men at the bars; I did my own thing and made it clear that I needed no one. Then, one day—*poof!*—it was true.

I had pulled off a kind of magic trick. I had perfected a sense of aloofness that masked, even to me at times, my desperate need for love. I had cemented, for a long time to come, my inability to have a normal relationship based on mutual love, trust, and respect. Since I had none of those feelings for myself, I certainly couldn't have them for someone else.

I WAS A DORK IN HIGH SCHOOL.

The possible labels were rock, jock, poindexter—and dork. The rocks took vocational classes and wore blue jean jackets and jeans and smoked cigarettes outside of the gym doors. The jocks were the athletes, or the cheerleaders, or the kids who dated the athletes or the cheerleaders. They dressed well, typically came from a family that was at least middle-income, and joined things like Ski Club and German Club. The poindexters were the smart kids, the ones who knew they were smart, and that being smart made them kind of uncool, and didn't care.

The dorks were the leftovers—not cool enough for the rocks, not athletic enough for the jocks, not confident enough for the poindexters. Some of them were just average, normal kids who went about the business of school, hung with their friends, and were unaffected by the social aspects of labels. I was not one of those people. I was affected by the labels. I was smart, unattractive, wore thick glasses, had bright red hair, and dressed poorly.

Even though my brothers and friends were not dorks, I remained one in their midst. One would think that the blanket of dorkiness would have lifted merely by associating with them, but no such luck. My brothers simply moved in different circles. And what happened with my friends was kind of a grandfather-clause effect; we became friends early on, before the social rules were set up and enforced. Then, when we got older and it became clear that I was going to be a dork, my friends, who were clearly going to be jocks, kept me, anyway. I loved them for that.

Also, because of this cross-clique inclusion phenomenon, I was able to move freely between the other dorks and the jocks. I was infinitely more comfortable among the dorks, for sure. The only pressure with them was for grades, and I could compete with that. The jocks were more like my dangling carrot; everything about them was just out of my reach, but I kept right on trying. I was a plucky little dork.

I was also very bright, averaging in at least the high nineties pretty much every semester. English was my strong suit, and in ninth grade I was allowed to jump into junior and senior English classes while still receiving credit for ninth grade English. Through it all, I managed to spend an exorbitant amount of time obsessing about the jocks and their little preppy monogrammed purses and how I might earn enough money to buy one and whether I would finally be cool or simply a dork with a nice purse.

I was a perpetual wannabe. I wanted to be cool enough for my brothers to respect me and want to hang with me. I wanted to be a good athlete so the other kids would respect me and want to hang with me. I wanted to be beautiful so the other girls would respect me and want to hang with me. I needed desperately to be included, and it was, in retrospect, probably that very desperation that ensured it would never happen.

So I was on the fringe, and I couldn't understand why my brothers were not. We all came from the same family, the same family situation, and yet they didn't seem to struggle with the issues that consumed me on a daily basis. They were popular, athletic, musical, smart, and confident. They had friends and hobbies and lives. It really seemed quite unfair. Of course, they didn't have OCD, so it was never a level playing field.

I took refuge in the bar down the street on weekend nights, hanging out with older kids so my age wouldn't be as easily questioned. Being drunk made me feel invincible; it numbed the shame that burned in my gut, soothed the exposed nerve that was my emotional state. Alcohol was like a smooth, silky shawl around the shards of self-doubt that threatened to deflate me at every turn.

I was pretty sure right off the bat that I had a drinking problem, though. They say that if you even question whether you might be an alcoholic, then you probably are one; social drinkers don't usually feel the need to ask.

DURING MY SENIOR YEAR IN HIGH SCHOOL, MY BRAIN TOOK A TURN FOR THE WORSE.

After leapfrogging past everyone but the seven people ranked ahead of me in just about every subject for the past ten years, I became stupid. I don't know how, although I'm inclined to believe the nightly drinking factored in. All I know for sure is that by the end of the first semester of my senior year, I was failing calculus and physics. Apparently, the alcohol went directly to the side of my brain that handles logic.

My eighteenth birthday, the day I turned legal, was in January of my senior year of high school. I spent the evening at one of the bars where I'd been drinking the past couple of years. As people bought me drink after drink to celebrate my big birthday, the bartender pretended not to notice that he'd been serving a minor all that time, and continuously served me White Russians, which tasted like vanilla milkshakes with a little kick. It was the little kick that got to me, and by midnight I was hammered.

What I remember goes something like this: I was too drunk to walk home, and my friends were too loaded to drive me home, so someone decided I should leave with a guy who, along with his twin brother, had quite the reputation as a ladies' man. The next thing I remember is being pushed up against the passenger door of his car with my pants down. Even though he was pushed against me, he was having some trouble, er, "performing," and finally he got pissed off and gave up.

I woke up in my own bed with a much clearer understanding of what it must feel like to be hit by a truck. My head was spinning and pounding, my body ached, and my privates were private no more. I hurt. And I was scared and angry and ashamed.

At about noon, I made my way downstairs where my mother was having coffee with a neighbor. They both agreed I looked horrible, and I went back to bed. When the neighbor left, I found my mother again.

"Mom," I said, forcing the words out of my mouth, "Can you tell the next day if you've had sex?"

I thought my mom should've been more alarmed with the question than she was, but she wasn't. "Yes, sometimes you can be sore for a day or two." Like this was a conversation we had all the time: mother and daughter chatting about sexual exploits. Except that we never had those chats.

As the day progressed, she must have realized that something wasn't right because she put me in the car and took me to see her gynecologist. It was my first time at such a doctor, an older male who made me very uncomfortable with his demeanor. After hearing my story, rather than examine me, he chose to lecture me instead. My mom and I sat in chairs facing his desk, both of us mortified as he extolled the dangers of excessive drinking and then sent us on our way.

I told my older brother about it, and he and his friends were all revved up to kick "the ladies' man's" ass—until I realized, seeing the twins in the bar the next week, that I didn't know which one it was who had tried to have sex with me. After a few drinks one night, I singled out the twin I thought was guilty and I yelled, "You could've gotten me pregnant!" He looked at me for a second, and then just walked away. I was dismissed.

My brother and his friends lost their passion for justice when they realized they would never know who hurt me, and I lost mine when I realized that it happened because I was drunk. I told myself the assault was my fault; I was to blame. The shame of this would have been unbearable had I not been so practiced in the art of avoidance.

After my birthday, the idea of going to school—walking the hallways, dragging through classes, talking to friends or to teachers—became unbearable. I couldn't concentrate, and most days I could barely get out of bed. Since English was the only subject of which we were required to take four years in order to graduate, and I had four of them due to the extra ninth-grade credit, it got worked out with the school that I would graduate mid-year. No one would have to know about my mental breakdown. I could retain my class ranking because I wouldn't officially fail anything, and I could have some time before college to decide whether I wanted to live. This worked out well for everyone, I think.

CHAPTER FIVE

BLUE BELT

"BLUE IS A SYMBOL OF THE SKY, WHICH THE YOUNG PLANT TRIES TO REACH. THE BLUE-BELT STUDENT FOCUSES HIS ENERGY ON ACHIEVING THE NEXT LEVEL."

~GWEN BRUNO, LIVESTRONG.COM

Blue belt is where we started learning to spar—to be fast, accurate, and defensive. I was a good fighter, quick and energetic. I gained a reputation as the one to beat in the point matches. The *katas* were more complicated and the self-defense moves more creative, and the better I did, the better I felt.

Sparring was the first sport at which I excelled, and it gave me a feeling that, at first, I was not comfortable with. I'd always avoided the spotlight because illumination could reveal all manner of flaws and imperfections; and I'd spent the better part of my life attempting to hide mine. The head gear combined with the sweat ensured no cover-up would stick to my skin or pencil marks to my eyebrows, and, for the first time in my life, I didn't care. At least, not as much. My love of sparring was stronger than my need to conceal my compulsions.

It was a small step for the young plant but a step nevertheless.

⁓

1980, AGE EIGHTEEN.

This sure is getting old, I think to myself as I come to. I'm just a freshman in college, and I'm already tired of it. I'm in a bathroom, having decided at some point during the evening that I'd always wanted to sleep next to a toilet and, damn it, tonight's the night. I shakily get to my feet, the hangover already so strong that I wish I could take off my head and carry it home in a grocery bag until it feels better.

I look around the bathroom for a couple of shot glasses filled with water because even when I'm blasted I usually remember to take out my contacts and store them in relative safety, but there are none to be found. Great, I think. That's just what I want to do right now; search the frat house.

I make my way out of the bathroom toward the kitchen. The smell in the house is overpowering—at least, I'm hoping it's the house and not me. It's a combination of urine, cigarettes, stale beer, and something fruity that I can't quite put my finger on. Oh, yes—now I recall: the punch in the garbage can. Damn that punch.

The smell of greasy food turns me back from the kitchen, and I head to the large, high-ceilinged rooms that make up the ground floor. There are bodies scattered on the couches and chairs, the occasional pledge curled up on the floor, and my guess is that most of these people won't be coming to until it's time to start partying again. But that's not me. I'm up. I have a day to attend.

I go from room to room in search of my contacts-in-a-shot-glass, quietly opening the doors, scanning dressers, and closing the doors. I come across couples who I know to be couples and a few who are, for lack of a better term, new friends, but I'm not here to judge. I'm here to find my goddamn contacts.

I enter a room at the end of the hall on the second floor, scan the dresser, and—voila!—the telltale shot glasses. I slip into the room, confirm that the glass on the right contains the contact with the dot for my right eye, gently pick them up, and turn to leave. There on the bottom bunk is a guy I know vaguely, a brother at the frat house, not someone I particularly care for. As I tiptoe by, my eye catches something familiar—my underpants are on the floor next to his bed. I know they're mine because they're day-of-the-week underpants and, besides being the only college freshman in the history of the world to wear day-of-the-week underpants, I'd had to wear the wrong day.

I look down my jeans and confirm the obvious, and look back at the boy on the bed. I snatch the panties up, stuff them in my pocket, take another look at the boy, and head back to the bathroom to vomit.

COLLEGE WAS, IN GENERAL, A GROWTH EXPERIENCE FOR ME.

It was the first time I'd been away from my parents and anyone else who knew me, the first time I could experiment with who and what I wanted to be. It was the first of many times I was able to start over and try to get it right, unaware that what was wrong with me, by definition, prevented a do-over from ever being successful. Instead, I spent those years discovering new manifestations of my OCD—hypochondria, for example—and perfecting my true dramatic roots, shocking my conservative, white parents at every family event with well-timed bombs: "Guess what? I'm dating a black guy!" or "Guess what? My roommate's a lesbian!" or "Guess what? I think *I'm* a lesbian!" Needless to say, the phrase "Guess what?" was met with trepidation after a while, and not a little eye-rolling.

I didn't really see myself as a lesbian, but part of me was crushed when my lesbian roommate was not interested in me. And I'd met a girl the first day of college whom I adored, who was my soul mate, my best friend, and who left me devastated when she left school the following spring because it was too staid and conservative for her. Maybe I wasn't in love with her, but it sure hurt when she was gone.

A friend and I took to haunting gay men's bars on weekends because nothing could be more fun than dancing with men who will never want to sleep with you. It was the perfect place for us to be: no rejection. Or, if you'd prefer, inherent but nonjudgmental rejection. Either way, it wasn't our fault. Unfortunately, due to the appalling shortage of gay men's bars in our little town, we spent much of our freshman year hitchhiking to a larger town about sixty miles away because it was so much more progressive, so much more liberal, and oh, so much more anonymous.

As I began developing the hypochondria, I turned my attention to the various diseases I was sure I had, checking off symptoms, and plotting a graph of how much longer I had to live. This required constant re-plotting because the darned diseases kept changing on me, but that was okay. It kept my head busy and supplied much-needed fuel to the informational bombs—the "Guess what?"—I felt I owed my parents. I was so intent on shocking them, and showing them how strong and cool and independent I was, that the one thing I should have told them— that I was dying inside, that there was something wrong with me, and that I needed help—was never said.

THERE IS A CERTAIN EXQUISITE PLEASURE IN PULLING A HAIR OUT BY THE ROOT.

For those of us looking for a momentary jolt of pain without drawing blood, nothing beats it. And, of course, once one eye's lashes are gone, you really have to do the other eye so they'll be even and, presumably, less conspicuous. The intellectual side of me has always been slightly amused by the crazy side and its ability to rationalize just about anything.

I looked up hair-pulling one day when I noticed my infant son playing with his eyelashes, and I panicked. By then, thank God, the Internet was around, and I immediately googled whether what I do, whatever it is, could be passed down to my children. I learned that it has a name, and that TTM was classified, back then, as an impulse control disorder. I sat at my computer and wept; there were support groups and chat rooms and anti-anxiety medication that would help, and, for the first time in my life, I didn't feel like a freak.

The more I read, the more frustrated I became that I hadn't checked into it sooner, or brought it up to my mother, to a friend, or to a therapist. And while anything with the word "mania" attached to it is kind of off-putting, at least it had a name. What I'd been doing to myself since grade school was a quantifiable, identifiable, recognized behavior.

In my research that day, I found that this particular type of disorder may or may not have a genetic component, but that the overlying tendencies can be inherited. I took this to mean that my son might have been born with the predisposition to obsessive-compulsive disorder, but that didn't mean he would definitely develop it, nor that one of the manifestations would automatically be hair-pulling. The funny part, in retrospect, is this: Even as I went through obsessive phases of buying, say, pillows or shoes, and knowing that my dad hoarded toiletries in his linen closet and had developed a healthy obsession with coupon clipping, and that one of my aunts was obsessed with cleaning, I still never made the heredity connection. The behaviors were too disparate to connect in my mind. And so it took years to determine that what I have is OCD.

I watched my son closely for several weeks afterward for any signs of the eyelash pulling, but it never reappeared.

THERE WAS GOOD NEWS ABOUT THIS DISCOVERY.

It was that I realized I wasn't making up the fact that I had something uncontrollable going on. And at least my eyebrows and eyelashes always grow back.

The bad news is that my eyebrows have been so chronically abused that they now grow back cowering in fear of me. They are so light as to be transparent, presumably in the hope that if I can't see them, I can't pluck them. And they are oddly and hopelessly sparse; one hair would need a bullhorn to make contact with its closest neighbor.

What this means in the real world is that I will no longer swim underwater and I will no longer walk in the rain because my penciled brows would wash off and I would look like a freak. These goals were easily enough met before I had my children but are a little more challenging lately since my kids seem to have a bizarre affinity for the water. Damn the luck.

I remember a fellow bartender at some dive bar downtown pulling me aside one night and advising me, as graciously as she could, that I shouldn't actually be drawing my eyebrows on as though my face were a paint-by-number. She showed me how to gently, and with short strokes, pencil them in to look a little more normal. I loved her for it—and quit the job that night out of embarrassment.

I had the bright idea one time that I could wear false eyelashes; certainly they'd come a long way since the Carol Channing look, right? I found a beauty supply store that carried them, and studied the different types and their instructions. Finally, I had to ask a clerk for some assistance.

"I guess I'm not understanding how to use these," I said. "Can't you just glue them onto the rims of your eyes?"

The clerk examined the package I'd thrust at her, looked back up at me, and said, somewhat bewildered, "Well, I mean, um, no. You use a washable glue to adhere them to your existing lashes. You can't glue something to your . . . skin."

My hopes for a normal appearance had just disappeared, and I was not happy. "You mean to tell me you have to have eyelashes in order to have false eyelashes?" I yelled. "Why would I need false eyelashes if I already had eyelashes?"

I stormed out, devastated, leaving behind a woman who had probably never, until that day, heard those words in the same sentence.

I remember a girl in college, whom I did not know, studying my face one day on the quad and mouthing the words, "I used to do that, too." I looked at her with my best, "I'm sure I don't know what you're talking about" look and walked away, only to go back to my room and cry my eyes out.

I STARTED BORROWING A FRIEND'S CAR TO GET TO WORK AND BACK.

During those first couple of years of college, I had a few extra off-campus jobs and needed the transportation. Typically, this would not have added drama, but my history with cars was not a good one. Like my predilection for obscure rituals, I'm like a magnet for crappy cars and for unbelievably stupid things that happen to crappy cars. If I honestly thought that there was a metaphor for my life, "crappy cars" would be that metaphor.

My first accident when I was a teenager wasn't so much an accident as an error in judgment resulting in the loss of my mom's muffler. She'd let me take the car to high school one day after I got my license, and my friend and I promptly ditched class to go cruising in the village and look for boys who might've skipped as well. In a stunning case of bad timing, as we were stopped at a light on Main Street, I looked in my rearview mirror and saw, back some ways but gaining fast, my mom pedaling after us on her bicycle.

"You have got to be kidding me," I muttered.

As soon as the light turned green, I made a left turn and then a sudden right into an alley that I never even knew existed. Once we came upon the railroad tracks—which sent us airborne for a good twenty feet because, of course, I didn't know they were there and was going too fast for plain pavement—I realized the possible error in my escape plan. As we landed and left the muffler and rear bumper in the dust, it was confirmed.

I spent the rest of the school year riding in a car with its bumper tied on with a coat hanger—driven by my mother.

My second accident, in my senior year of high school, was worse. Three girls, not one of whom was really my friend, and I carpooled to look at colleges for a weekend. The car, belonging to the father of one of the girls, had a standard transmission, which I was very confident with in a parking lot but not quite as experienced with on the open road. My turn at the wheel was during a downpour, and between unnecessarily downshifting and hydroplaning, the car ended up against a guardrail at the top of a steep incline.

Fortunately, no one was hurt, but the damage to the car was extensive, and, of course, had to be paid for by my parents. If the girls and I weren't close before the trip, we were *really* not close afterward.

My next car experience—with a friend's car—presented a great argument for why people with no common sense should not be allowed to drive.

My plan for the holidays during my sophomore year of college was to work a few nights into Christmas break at my part-time bartending job before going home, and since I was going to miss hitching a ride with any of my classmates from the area, a friend who was staying on campus was kind enough to lend me her car for the break. It was a basic blue four-door sedan. I felt pretty confident I could handle it.

My older brother was graduating mid-year from another college a couple of hours away, and I graciously volunteered to drive there the day before I was leaving for home and bring a load of his stuff with me. The trip there was uneventful enough, and he loaded up as much as he could squeeze in.

The car was packed to the roof with boxed stereo equipment, albums, pretty much everything he owned. And, of course, his guns, which were in the trunk. As a hunter and a trapper, his gun collection was his pride and joy. Most of his possessions were high-end, purchased with the proceeds of an insurance settlement from a woman who'd driven her car into him on his motorcycle a few years previously.

On the way back to my school, I had to stop to use a bathroom in a little family restaurant, and promptly locked the keys in the car. By the time the locksmith arrived, I was way behind schedule and not a little pissed off. I had to work that evening at the bar, and I was going to be late. When I finally did get back to town, I didn't have time to take my brother's stuff to the friend's house where I was staying while the dorms were closed over break. She had already left for her job at another bar across the county line, which was open an hour later than mine, so I called her and agreed to run over after work and pick up her house key.

While I was working, I parked the car right outside—right on the sidewalk, in fact. It never left my sight, and I was quite pleased with my ingenuity, it being a rather questionable part of town and all. When I closed up, I drove to my girlfriend's bar, which was jam-packed. I parked, ran in, found her behind the bar, got the apartment key, stayed for one drink, and ran out.

And it was all gone.

All of it. The stereo equipment, the guns . . . gone.

I couldn't process it. The worst that could happen had happened, and there was no way to make it right. I actually considered killing myself, thinking that might be the only apt punishment. I already felt dead inside at the thought of having to tell him, my brother whom I loved more than life, whom I wanted to please more than my mom, whose opinion of me mattered more than anyone's. And for someone who's most persistent obsessive thought is the fear of someone being angry with her, I couldn't have screwed up more.

I called my mom the next morning and she broke the news to him before I got home. He didn't speak to me for many, many, many months. The cost of the broken window in the car was miniscule compared to the cost of the damage to my relationship with my brother and the damage to my own already flawed psyche.

THE NEXT SUMMER, I TOOK A JOB TENDING BAR AT THE SCENE OF THE CRIME.

Part of me believed I could find my brother's stuff; every once in a while a customer would whisper that they'd heard so-and-so had the stereo equipment or someone else had a rifle; eventually the incident was forgotten or—in my case—blocked out. But it turned out to be a better bar, job-wise, than the dive next to the bus station I'd started at, and so I stayed on even after my mission: unaccomplished. I was between my sophomore and junior years of college, it was a great place to work, and I took to hanging out with the owner after hours. He had a girlfriend who had moved to California, and, while he pined away for her during the day, I was hanging out with him at night. It was a lovely arrangement: he was old enough to be my father, which drew me to him, and he wasn't looking for a commitment.

Unfortunately, I started getting a little too comfortable and showing up to work hammered because I was the boss's squeeze and thought I could, and he didn't take too kindly to it. Pretty soon I was no longer working *or* being squeezed. I kept journals all through college, and there were entries that suggested I had a drinking problem and should probably try to stop drinking. I didn't. I did at least continue to realize and acknowledge the problem.

Around that time, I also started writing a column for the college newspaper. Every week, I'd write a few hundred words about whatever was bothering me that week on campus or in Washington or in the world at-large. I started honing my irony and sarcasm skills, tools that I eventually recognized as the first socially acceptable coping devices I'd ever adopted. Unfortunately, even those methods don't solve the inherent problem of the black hole where an ego should be, but they're much more fun for everyone.

By my third year of college, I couldn't take it anymore. The eyelash issue was in full bloom; I remember because toward the end of those three years, I couldn't wear my contacts sometimes since there were no lashes on my eyelids to grab so that I could put them in. In fact, contacts made the plucking worse. I'd put them in, and after a while my eyes would start to feel dry; I thought that plucking the lashes would make them feel better. Once I started, I couldn't stop until they were all gone, and then I had the darnedest time getting my contacts out because my process involved pulling the outer corners of my eyes—by the lashes—to pop the contacts out. No lashes made that very difficult.

I felt simultaneously caged and directionless. I'd started smoking in an effort to lose my "freshman fifteen," and was buying the gallon-jug size of cheap wine a few times a week. On Thursday nights, which were post-classes and pre-weekend, I would spend the evening sitting on my dorm windowsill overlooking the campus, drinking wine and smoking cigarettes and asking my journal why I hadn't killed myself yet. I would, later in life, throw away those journals for fear my children would find them one day and think I was quite nuts.

In one last burst of academic accomplishment, I achieved an almost unattainable goal. The single most important and difficult requirement for graduation at my school was the Baccalaureate Essay, a complex research paper that had to be passed by two out of three professors in order to graduate. If you didn't pass the essay, you remained at school for at least another semester. You were there until you passed it, if you wanted to leave with a degree. There were thirty-year-old students walking around campus still trying to pass the goddamn essay. And the proposal process for the essay was almost as excruciating; the essay topic had to be researched, outlined, and submitted within a certain period of time in the fall of one's senior year, and all of that had to be passed as well.

When it became clear to me, during the fall of my junior year, that I would not survive another year at college, dropping out was not an option. I'd invested too much money and heartache to leave without a degree in hand. Instead, I begged for and received permission to submit my essay proposal as a junior, and passed it. I then spent the winter writing the essay and passed that, too. I graduated in May, a year early.

I'D ALWAYS WONDERED WHERE THE HYPOCHONDRIA CAME FROM.

Was it endemic to any particular sort of people? For instance, would I have still been a hypochondriac if I wasn't an alcoholic? I know many other alcoholics and I don't think any of them think they have any one of a dozen fatal illnesses at any given time. So that wasn't the connection. I then wondered about people with low self-esteem. Are they generally hypochondriacs? What about anorexics? I could never find the common thread, until the concept of OCD came into my life. Then it all made sense; it's simply another obsessive thought. There's not necessarily a corresponding compulsion or ritual; it's just a thought that I can't seem to shake.

It doesn't help that I've always looked for the drama in life. I used to say, "When I die tragically young," blah, blah, blah. Now it's, "When I die tragically middle-aged," which I am convinced I will. And it's not easy being a hypochondriac either. It takes a lot of hard work, a lot of time off work for doctors' appointments, and a lot of mental anguish—from the highs ("I think I really *have* something this time!") to the lows ("What do you mean, it's just a plain bruise? Have you *ever* seen a bruise that color before?!")

It's exhausting. It's not a heavy period; it's ovarian cancer. I don't have an odd cranial structure; I have a brain tumor. It's not the flu; it's non-Hodgkin's lymphoma. Once, in my mid-twenties, I'd picked at a pimple on my cheek so badly that it was infected. I saw an ad for a free skin cancer screening clinic and high-tailed it down there because I was sure that's what it was, despite the fact that I knew I'd picked at it and made it the way it was. That's what obsessive thoughts can do: completely override your common sense.

The only thing I can figure about it—because, contrary to popular belief, I do have other things to do than worry about dying and wonder, myself, why I do it—is that physical pain, as opposed to emotional pain, is at least quantifiable. It's tangible. It's recordable. It means there's a concrete thing wrong with me that maybe can be fixed, at least when it really exists. The problem with obsessive thoughts, of which hypochondria is one, is that they seem real to us. All the logic in the world can't make us stop thinking that these thoughts are real. So sometimes I think we want them to be real so we don't *seem* like hypochondriacs. Again, it's a vicious cycle. It's not all *Monk* in the OCD world. As curious as it may be to watch someone with an obsessive need to wash his hands, I wish people were more aware of just how debilitating that need can be. It would be like telling someone with an excruciating itch that they're not allowed to scratch it.

Yet, with all of my anxiety over diseases that I was sure at one time or another were going to kill me, I'm extraordinarily healthy. My first real illness came in the form of mononucleosis in ninth grade; it was a major letdown, considering how long I'd waited for a genuine disease to afflict me. I had to stay home and sleep for two weeks, and all the while I was Peggy Lee, singing "Is That All There Is?" No one cared. No one sent flowers. There was no sympathy from most of the family ("Hey, all she does is sleep, anyway; how do you know she's even sick?"), except my younger brother, of course. He waited on me. My little buddy. My Gilligan.

When I didn't have any physically painful excitement going on in my life, I would make it up. I would jump really hard on my own bent ankle, hoping to sprain or—*better yet!*—break it.

I would twist my wrist as hard as I could for as long as I could, hoping for the same thing. I would purposely fall while roller skating, or slam into the wall to stop myself. Nothing ever broke. It was as if I were made of rubber.

One night in college, after many, many beers and a vodka and Diet Coke or two, I sat in the middle of the quad with my best guy friend and sobbed because I thought I was going blind. Poor David. He'd always end up walking me back to my dorm room, where I would proceed to strip in front of him, just to make him nuts, and climb into bed. He transferred out during his second year. He said it was because he wasn't getting the education he wanted; I supposed it was also so he didn't have to watch me self-destruct anymore. That was at least a nice bonus for him, I would imagine.

CHAPTER SIX

GREEN BELT

"Green signifies growth, just as a seed bursts forth from the earth and sends up leaves. Green-belt students have a firm foundation of martial arts knowledge on which to build as they practice and refine their skills."

~Gwen Bruno, Livestrong.com

I became a little more humble at green belt. We were now sparring with the upper belts and getting our asses handed to us with some frequency, and I realized there was still a ways to go. I knew all the moves, all the strikes, all the defensive maneuvers, but simply knowing the right way to do something doesn't necessarily make it easy to do.

That part takes practice.

1983, AGE TWENTY-ONE.

It has got to be 120 degrees out here. I'm sitting on this curb with my little clipboard laying next to me, smoking a Marlboro Light, and desperately wishing I had a drink. Doesn't even have to be alcohol. Water, soda, anything. I've still got two hours to go in this development of houses that mirrors the development of houses on either side of it, all with names of flowers or trees or some such shit: "Peony Farms" and "Lily Manor" and "Good God, do you realize all these houses look alike? Crossing."

I know this because I have been to each house in each development over the course of the day, ringing doorbells, preparing for the spiel: "Hi, I'm Maggie Lamond from CalPIRG, the California Public Interest Research Group! I'm here today to talk to you about [insert cause here] and to ask for your support." For a person such as myself, who is terrified of strangers and of public speaking, this is quite a spot to be in.

I'm here, of course, because of a guy. Matt. Matt and Howie, actually. I have been frustratingly stalled in my job search since I've been out here, and I finally answered an ad that's in the paper every freakin' day, meaning there's a pretty high turnover. But I need rent money; their turnover can't be my problem.

When I went to their office for an interview, I was both surprised and devastated that Matt knew my oldest brother from college. "I go all the way to California and I'm still my brother's sister?" I joked. But I wasn't really joking because Matt was one of the most attractive men I'd ever met, and now there was no way he would go out with me; I was my brother's little sister. Nevertheless, I took the job to pay my rent, sex life be damned.

On weekends, we drive down to Santa Cruz, five or six of us stuffed into a two-door, and spend the days playing Frisbee and swimming and giving each other foot rubs. At night, we sleep on the beach and, while I'm totally into the idea of it, I always find myself praying I wake up in the morning, alive and intact. I don't know what frightens me more: sea creatures or land creatures.

I just know that I really, really like hotels.

I DRAMATICALLY LEFT FOR CALIFORNIA A WEEK AFTER GRADUATING FROM COLLEGE.

The drama had long since been embedded in my overachieving and need-to-flee roots. It wasn't difficult, really; my parents and I were barely speaking due to an argument the day of my graduation. My graduating class protested the commencement speaker, whom my parents liked. She was pro-life and anti-birth-control and, basically, in our privileged, protesting eyes, against everything our little liberal college was for.

Besides, our class had voted for Andy Rooney and was overruled, so we were ticked off. We wore little white armbands and calmly filed out of the outdoor tent when the speaker was introduced, and filed back in when she was finished. And my parents filed back home, disgusted with the trash-talking, rabble-rousing, protesting-for-the-sake-of-protesting daughter they'd raised. I read it slightly differently, that is, that they'd always raised me to stand up for what I believed in, and now it turned out that they meant only if they believed in it too, and I was righteously indignant. I borrowed $700 from a rich classmate and left for California the following week. Starting over was just what I needed, I was sure.

I temporarily moved in with my older brother in Sacramento, who was beginning to speak to me again after I'd lost his most important possessions when the car got broken into. We tried to work it out, but our relationship remained strained and, after a few weeks, I found an apartment with two other women several miles away. My roommates were gay and lovers to boot, so once again I was the outsider. I had no vehicle and learned to use the bus system to get around while I job-hunted and found some good bars in which to recover after a hard day of searching. But money was tight.

After interviewing with two back-east guys from CalPIRG, I thought, *This is it. My new life is starting; the old one is gone.* I was finally getting another chance. Everything bad was in the past; nothing but good days lay ahead. The pisser about it all—the OCD and alcoholism—is that you can't simply choose not to have them anymore; I didn't choose to have them in the first place. Anxiety comes back, triggering the obsessive thoughts, triggering the compulsions, and, in my case, triggering the need to pick up a drink, and thereby triggering depression. I felt like a hamster again: I kept trying to get away from myself, but every time I looked back, there I was.

I tried to make money with CalPIRG but was just really, really bad at it. I was never good at asking for money, even from people I knew and even when it was owed to me. Borrowing the money to get to California was one of the hardest things I'd ever done, but that was how desperately I needed to run away. Knocking on strangers' doors and asking for money was excruciating for me, despite the good cause, and it left me no time to search for a better job. I flirted with going back to school, spent some afternoons at some local college bars, and called my old college friends, wasted, with stories of how good my life was on the West Coast. They were all having boring summers, working and getting ready for senior year, and looking to me for their vicarious adventures. I did the best I could with the imagination I had.

After three months, the back-east guys were moving back east, and I went with them, moving back home. It was too sunny in California to accommodate my moods, anyway.

AFTER THE DEBACLE OF CALIFORNIA, I COULDN'T STAY HOME EITHER.

The relationship between my parents and me had become even more strained as a result of my abrupt departure and return.

It was October, and what would have been my senior year in college was in full swing. I headed back there, to my college, and lived with friends for a couple of months, pretending the whole time that I was glad I wasn't a student anymore. After overstaying my welcome by several weeks—because my friends were, in fact, still students and had work to do—I researched my options and determined that I had exactly one left. I fled to the city where my best male friend had transferred and was finishing school. I moved in with him and his girlfriend and roommate. They still had one year left; they hadn't felt the need to "Start life!" as I had, and were comfortably ensconced in campus life. For the record, I probably left college because I actually couldn't afford another year. "Starting life!" just sounded so much more . . . fun.

There I was, starting over again, hanging out with my best friend and his girlfriend, who may or may not have understood our relationship, and wildly attracted to his roommate—or, rather, his roommate's cologne. Many a night we'd hit the clubs and drink and dance until closing, and many a night the guys would hoist me into the roommate's little Saab, get me home, and hoist me into bed, where I cried yet again over my rejected advances.

One night, I was walking through campus, the smell of fall and the crunch of leaves under my feet making me ache to go back in time—back to college, back to high school, back to some time when I wasn't so emotionally black and blue. I knew it wasn't going to happen, of course, but the ache was consuming me. I stopped at a bar somewhere on campus and got drunk, then found a hill I could throw myself down in an effort to break a bone. That didn't work, so I started twisting my wrist with all of my strength, falling on it, twisting it again, falling on it again, until it was red and swollen. I then went to the emergency room, where I was admitted—not for a broken wrist but for dehydration from alcohol poisoning. My friend came and picked me up a few hours later, after I'd eaten every available ice chip in the hospital.

The girlfriend took it for about as long as any reasonably smart young woman could, and, after a month or so, it was gently suggested that I needed to find my own place. Coincidentally, a girl from my college town, whom I'd been friends with years earlier, was moving close by; we hooked up as roommates in the college section of the city. It was going to be great—two single girls, partying away, having fun. "This is it," I remember telling myself and my parents. *This* is when my life will start.

And it did start—taking a turn for the worse. As a fixture at the college bar down the street, I spent many a night getting blasted with the townies who recognized me for what I was: a non-college outsider. I had never gotten along well with college kids, even when I was one, and so instead I found a kind of easy camaraderie with a couple of other fringe patrons. I was a smart ass when I was sober, and worse when I was loaded—"I'm a non-student and proud of it, goddamn it!"—and so there was more than one memorable evening spent screaming in the parking lot or throwing bottles against the nearby grocery store's brick walls. To this day I am both grateful and not a little amazed that I was never arrested.

MY HAIR ISSUES AT THIS POINT WERE IN FULL BLOOM.

There would be times when I plucked my eyebrows until they bled, and my roommate once tactfully offered me her tweezers. My burning embarrassment at being busted once again led to accelerated abuse, not to mention a strong determination to get better at the plucking process. As I got better at it, as I learned to appreciate and then compulsively crave the smoothness of the hairless eyebrow, there was no more blood drawn. So there you go. On the one hand, practice makes perfect; on the other, be careful what you wish for.

The bar down the street became my home away from home. It was convenient, and it had beer and shuffleboard. There really wasn't much more I needed in life. The students who hung out at the bar took to viewing me with not a little disdain, as if I were so much garbage sitting at the bar waiting for Mr. Right. It was laughable, really; all I wanted was to get drunk and watch people. I didn't want anything from them except maybe to pick up a few pointers on how to blend in.

I took to wearing a fake diamond ring at the bar and telling people that I was engaged to a guy who went to school in another state. Sometimes I'd turn the fake-diamond side toward my palm, leaving only the fake gold band exposed, and tell people I was married. Sometimes I said I was widowed or going through a divorce. All the time I lied. My theory was that if people thought I had some valid connection to a legitimate life, a life away from the barstool on which I sat when I wasn't playing shuffleboard or dancing, then as far as they were concerned I was okay. They didn't need to know that I was just biding my time, waiting for the pause in my current life to end so my real life could start.

One night a guy was standing next to me at the bar, looking down at my head and my face. "Did you have cancer?" he asked.

I realized he was talking about my hair, or, more accurately, the places my hair used to be. It had been a stressful few months, and my lashes and brows took the brunt of the suffering. Apparently, the hair on my head had started to thin some, too, although I don't remember including it in my obsession. Maybe it was just falling out in a dramatic show of solidarity.

"Yes, I do," I replied. "I've recently finished chemo and radiation, and they're hoping it's all gone."

"Wow," he said. "That's weird. I mean, 'cause your hair didn't fall out like other people's hair who have cancer and shit. Are you sure you had cancer?" He then elbowed his buddy, and they both walked away snickering. The shame was again hammered home. And again, it didn't occur to me to wonder if anyone else did what I did. That's how intrinsically sure I was that no one did.

During my first year in the city, I started over a lot. I lived in eight different apartments in the university section. The place I shared with my college friend became emotionally uninhabitable after the eyebrow situation was exposed, and I moved out. Another time, the landlord sold the house, and a third move was the result of my new dog, who shit all over the floor and ruined the rugs. He was soon my former dog, and it was years before I was mature and responsible enough to have a pet again.

I just couldn't stop looking for ways to start anew.

They weren't all bad experiences either, those apartments. There were always people looking for roommates in the university area, so finding one was never difficult, although finding one with whom I was compatible was something of a challenge. One roommate in a two-bedroom flat had a baby and a parrot the size of a dog. It was a toss-up every night to see which would keep me up longer.

Another perpetually perky young woman came out of the shower one morning and said, "Mmmmmm! Don't you just love shaving your legs?!" I thought she was joking—because I had, in fact, never met a woman who likes shaving her legs—and replied, "Yep! It's right up there with root canals in terms of just plain fun!" She frowned and left the room; we weren't roommates much longer. I lived with men, women, students, professionals, addicts, athletes, musicians, and a family in the space of that year.

I suppose, it could all be attributed to my need for drama and crises to distract me from focusing on what was most important: the fact that I was suicidally unhappy. I had no direction, no focus, no drive except to get away from myself and my inability to control my thoughts and compulsions. It turns out that one of the best ways to break an obsessive thought is through distraction, so, in a way, I was instinctively doing what I needed to do to survive.

Starting over was becoming a career, and one I was not very good at.

AT TWENTY-TWO, I FOUND MYSELF INEXPLICABLY UNEMPLOYED.

My sole job-seeking credentials included a liberal arts college degree and experience in serving beer, so looking for work was a demeaning process. There wasn't exactly a liberal arts store or a liberal arts office where I could get a job, and any chance I had of working at a bar was shot when I unfailingly sat at the bar and got blasted after the interview. Boy, the things they don't teach you at liberal arts schools. I'm still bitter.

I eventually started working as a secretary for a truck dispatcher, thanks to a friend of my dad who had a trucking company in a nearby city. It was not a pleasant job, as truck stops are not historically enriching work environments for reasonably attractive young women, but it was a paycheck, and it provided compelling daily validation for me to keep abusing myself. *If I pick at my face, maybe I won't be attractive and the men won't look at me like that. If I get really thin, maybe I'll just blend into the desk*—if, if, if. If I knew why I needed to do those things, maybe I could have stopped.

I drove the ten miles to work every day in a 1972 Dodge Dart that my parents helped me buy. It had no heat, and it was mid-January in the northeast. I was too busy scraping frost off the inside of the windshield while cruising down the highway to notice that a car had broken down and stopped up ahead. I ran into it at about fifty miles per hour with no seatbelt and walked away with only a sprained wrist and a few bruised ribs, continuing the embarrassing trend of surviving things that should really have killed me. Three years later, the occupants of the stalled car walked away with a hundred thousand dollars from my insurance company. A little something for their trouble— and as an apology for my almost killing them. While it was not anywhere close to my last car accident, it was, thankfully, my last lawsuit.

While recuperating from that mishap, I developed pneumonia and spent a couple of weeks sleeping in a recliner because the coughing hurt my ribs and I didn't cough quite as much sitting up. Every time I tried to eat, a coughing fit would bring the food back up again, introducing me to yet another resource I had been unaware of: bulimia. I realized that after vomiting, I felt clean again—thin and clean. When the pneumonia cleared up, I'd lost twenty pounds and realized I could eat anything I wanted and not gain weight as long as I stuck my fingers down my throat within a reasonable period of time.

At this time, I was living in a basement apartment of a house owned by a professor and her family. The apartment had no windows and no separate entry; I had to walk into their foyer and turn right to hit the basement stairs. Once down there, I felt as if I were in my own little bat-cave. It was dark and cool and cozy—womb-like even. It was a perfect place to be depressed, and I often celebrated that by making myself puke in the little toilet they'd installed down there.

This was easy to do most of the time because I still had a bad leftover cough from the pneumonia. All I had to do was eat and start a coughing fit before the food digested. Since I barely had to use my fingers, I reasoned it couldn't logically be called bulimia. Bulimics put their fingers down their throats on a regular basis. I was different; I only did it when there was no available cough. We alcoholic, body-fixated, obsessive-compulsive people are nothing if not fabulous rationalizers. Ask any of us.

Bulimia was an intriguing experience for me; the results were so immediate. The results of starving can take days to be evident. Though I cringed at the thought of vomiting, the feeling when I was done was nothing short of euphoric. I was clean again; I could start over. There was nothing in there to add weight or to make me feel full. Every time I puked, I felt like I owned the world. I was in charge. It was all mine. Saying it now makes it seem silly, but that's what it felt like: When I puked, I was king.

MY BOSS AT THE TRUCK STOP WAS VERY ANXIOUS TO SUCCEED IN THE WORLD OF DISPATCHING.

Though older than me, he was still a young guy and a former long-distance driver who'd switched to the truck stop because he wanted to settle down with his wife and have kids and all that. I admired his enthusiasm and dedication and glommed onto him as a father figure to rescue me from the world I could not seem to flee. Convinced that I never ate, he always bought me lunch at the diner by the truck stop, and when I had my car accident, he came and picked me up at the hospital and brought me home.

He and his wife invited me to their house for a few holidays, where we would watch a new music video channel called MTV. We had dinners together, went to a couple of movies, and generally hung out. They quickly became a surrogate family. I didn't hate my job specifically because this guy was there. He looked out for me, right up until the time he tried to seduce me on his desk.

At that point, I figured he wasn't looking out for me anymore. His wife figured out the same thing, and, before I knew it, he was back driving a truck and I was without a boss.

It turned out that our little slice of truck stop heaven was closing anyway, and I was unceremoniously moved by my new, out-of-town boss to another local truck stop that had a reputation for being a little more than a truck stop. I was always reminded of the old hockey joke: "I went to a fight and a hockey game broke out," substituting "brothel" and "truck stop" for "fight" and "hockey game." Typically, the women working at that particular truck stop were looking for "dates" outside in the trucks rather than loads of freight for the drivers. The good news was that I was given my own office—no more men to answer to in the immediate vicinity. There was one other woman with an office in the building, and the rest of the trucking companies represented up and down the hallways of the truck stop were managed by men. The other woman worked across the hall and took me under her wing. I was twenty-two years old—old enough to not need such protection, probably, but not really.

I could do the work, but the drivers and the other dispatchers were a challenge. They saw a woman in a truck stop and their first thought was not usually *boss*. And I knew why; I'd seen the women who prowled the parking lot. I also knew I wasn't one of them, regardless of the very fine line that separated us.

I went out drinking every night after work, stayed out until the bars closed at 2:30 a.m., rolled out of bed at 7:40 a.m., drove down the highway with my eyes barely open, and was at my desk by eight o'clock. Like my father, I never missed a day of work because of a hangover. Unlike my father, I rarely showered in the mornings because that would involve getting out of bed ten minutes earlier, and I have to assume that some mornings my office actually smelled like the bar I'd left mere hours earlier. This did nothing to convince the drivers that I was on the up-and-up, but it didn't matter because, the trucking industry being unstable at the time, my office closed as well.

I was then offered a job by a man down the hall, one of the more successful people in the field. I soon found that one of the reasons he was so good was his salesmanship. He could convince a driver to take a load of paper 800 miles out of his way and feel privileged to do so. He was powerful and charming, and everyone wanted to be on his good side. Everyone wanted to be his friend. If it were college, he would have been the "big man on campus."

I just wanted a paycheck until I could figure out my next move. The workplace involved a lot more groping and grabbing than even I was accustomed to, however, and I found myself in panic mode most hours of the day—I needed the job, I needed the paycheck, I needed to be able to respect myself, and I needed my boss to not be mad at me.

ONE OF MY JOBS FOR HIM WAS TO DO HIS ERRANDS, INCLUDING HIS BANKING.

After a few such banking visits, I befriended the branch manager of the bank, who I believed was everything I was not but wanted to be: professional. He wore suits and managed a bank, for God's sake; can't get much more professional than that. He was the seemingly requisite ten to fifteen years older than me that I needed, and so I agreed to go out for drinks one night after work. He took me to a little bar that would eventually become my second home. It was a hole-in-the-wall blues place that had open mike on Wednesdays and bands on the weekends, and, while there, I fell in love—with the bar.

The guy was another story. While not exactly my type, he was kind to me, and I felt classy in his presence. In keeping with the persistent rebound relationship mentality that consumed me, I thought, *This is it. This will be the one. He will fill the hole in my heart.* We dated a few times, and I kept expecting him to ask me to spend the night—but nothing. I thought to myself, *Well, isn't this nice. He's a gentleman. He's waiting until the right time . . .* and waiting and waiting and waiting.

Apparently, the right time just never presented itself because he never made a pass at me. Most of the time he was wasted, and I blamed his inability to appreciate my charm on the alcohol, which seemed to make sense for a while. Then one day, he asked me to accompany him to an out-of-town wedding close to my hometown, and I was thrilled. He bought me a classy new outfit and new shoes—the most expensive shoes I had ever owned. I remember this part because several months later the heel fell off the shoe, and, for some reason, that made me feel smug and righteous. At the time, I felt stunning. We drove to the wedding and made our way to the reception at a hotel afterward. I was nervous and anxious, being in a crowd of people I didn't know, and tried to monitor my drinking because of it. My date, however, got blasted.

After a couple of hours, we were standing next to each other at the bar, each chatting with the person on our other side. The next thing I knew, my date began shouting at me, accusing me of flirting with the man I'd been talking to. I tried reassuring him that this was not, in fact, the case, as did the poor man at my side, but he would not be reassured. Then I was following him to the front desk, begging him to believe me, and watching him check out of the hotel.

I followed him up to the room. He packed his things and told the bellman on the way out that I was, under no circumstances, allowed to stay in the room for the night. The reservation was under his name, and he had paid for it, and he didn't want me to have access to it. He then left the hotel, got in his car, and drove away. It was 2:30 a.m.

The bellman and I stood there for a moment in silence. I was completely lost as to what to do, not to mention as close as I'd ever been to a full-blown anxiety attack. I was not even imagining that someone was mad at me; someone actually *was* mad—furious, in fact. My self-hatred was validated.

I had no money of my own and no car. As I stood in the hotel room with the bellman who had been instructed to throw me out, tears were streaming down my face. I started shaking and hyperventilating, crossing that elusive border into panic from which the bellman probably knew I wouldn't return any time soon; he finally conceded the room key and left.

The next morning, I called my parents, who lived a half hour from the hotel. By this point in my life, my mother had learned not to ask many questions of me unless she really wanted the answers. She came to the hotel, took her hung-over, pathetic excuse for a daughter to the bus station, bought me a ticket, and sent me on my way. Between the man who left me at the hotel and the disappointment I saw in my mother's eyes, I was dangerously close to the edge. My innate sense of self-preservation kicked in, though, and I lived.

CHAPTER SEVEN

BROWN BELT

"Brown is a symbol of the ripening and maturing of a plant. The brown-belt student is gaining the maturity necessary to advance to the highest levels. He is reaping the benefits of hard work."

~Gwen Bruno, Livestrong.com

We had to start running at brown belt; to achieve black belt, the student, or *senpai*, is required to run three miles in twenty-four minutes. Our instructor kept track of our efforts after class each day. I had never run in my life, except that day when I was eleven and ran around the house thirty times to burn off a candy bar.

I started by running around my block. Then I worked up to twice around my block. One day, I realized I was running three miles and making my time, and had become, in my thirties, something of an athlete. I was thin but muscular, my arms and legs no longer belonged to a stick figure, and I was healthy again—and possibly for the first time in my adult life.

1987, AGE TWENTY-FIVE.

I recently got my first job at a small law firm, and my boyfriend has surprised me with three new suits and a leather briefcase. He is so proud of me; he knew, as I did on some level, that although I love doing it and am quite good at it, I am not destined to spend my life tending bar. This is where my new life begins.

We live together in a two-bedroom flat, for which we bought second-hand furniture that I love dearly because it is ours. Our living room sports an oversized and only slightly used sectional sofa. For the kitchen, I found a retro-looking dinette set and discount dishes. The pièce de résistance, however, is in the dining room: an old oak claw foot table on which I serve my boyfriend the dinners I make every night when I get home from work.

In the beginning, when we first moved in here and started plotting our future together, I couldn't have been happier. I was with a man who made me feel safe and loved and working in a field that I found challenging and exciting. I'd succeeded in prying myself from the bluesy bar that had become my second home, from people who were my second family, in an effort to secure the stable, sane future for which I yearned.

As the months have worn on, though, something has changed. The more time I spend in the office, with people who are not drunk half the time and who share similar interests and goals, the more frustrated I am when I get home. I don't like cooking dinner every night. I loved the idea of domesticity, but it's not me, not now. Once again, I'm posing. I'm trying on a new reality, a new start, and finding, once again, that it doesn't quite fit.

It breaks my heart because I do believe I love him. Flawed though it's been, this is my first serious relationship, reciprocal and somewhat equal. But every day, I'm becoming less tolerant of his drunken friends coming and going, less tolerant even of his own drunken comings and goings. There may be a day that I'm not going to want to drink anymore—maybe I'll want to have a baby—and I don't think I can be here and be sober. As I look around at the apartment I love, the furniture I've made my own, my upright piano that he proudly listens to me play, I'm beginning to see, ever so slowly and painfully, that my new life will have to begin somewhere else. There will be no happy ending here; rationally, I had known there was never going to be.

LIFE WENT ON AT THE TRUCK STOP.

A couple of the drivers started treating me like a daughter, looking out for me a little bit, and were none too happy when my boss belittled or ridiculed me in their presence. I had learned to accept it as part of the territory until the glorious day that I realized I deserved better. That day I grabbed my purse and fled. I'd tried to hold out until I had my paycheck in hand, but couldn't.

Jobless and paycheck-less, I went to the only bar I knew well enough to feel safe, where the man from the bank had brought me. It was the middle of the afternoon and no one was around except the owner of the place, whom I'd met on previous occasions. He was a giant of a man, six foot seven or more, and a genuinely nice, authentic guy. He was sitting on a stool at the end, and we began talking. Crying, I shared my tale of woe, and this man, my new hero, drove to the truck stop to collect my last check. Then he hired me. Thus began the second chapter of my bartending experience. It was May, and I was twenty-three. It was the springtime of my life.

Around that time, my favorite uncle, my mother's brother, told us he had AIDS. Andy was wise, funny, and talented; he was my role model, my idol, my mentor. A one-time monk, he dropped out of the order to get married, and then got divorced. He was gay, but no one in the family knew it, or, if they did, they kept it to themselves. He was a writer and an editor who lived in a fabulous apartment on Manhattan's Upper West Side, and he lived the life I wanted to live—except, of course, for the priest, marriage, divorce, and gay parts.

He always came home for Thanksgivings, and that previous year had been no exception. Something was clearly going on, however; the difference was in his tone, his appearance, and his usual "Uncle Al, the kiddies' pal" persona, which was now somewhat subdued. It wasn't until after the holidays that he broke the news to us. We were all devastated, both by the diagnosis and its implication; at the time, it was broadly assumed that AIDS was spread two ways only: gay sex or intravenous drug use. We were pretty sure he didn't do drugs; he was too high on life to need any boosting.

Also at this point in time, the mid-eighties, people were just beginning to grasp the finality of an HIV diagnosis. There were no AIDS "cocktails," no pills, no vaccines in the works. People who tested positive could only focus on diet, nutrition, and exercise to get the most out of the time they had left. Since homosexuality is not high on the list of good Catholic traits, my mom and dad surprised everybody—including themselves, I think—by asking Uncle Andy to come and live with them and let them take care of him. I remember asking my dad about this, and he said, "Well, what are we going to do? It's Andy." Yet another surprise.

THE BAR WAS THE PERFECT SETUP FOR ME.

I was getting paid to drink with my friends. We'd do shots behind the bar, and, come closing time, if we weren't already loaded, we'd stay until we were, goddamn it. I'd usually drive home blasted in the wee hours of the morning, sleep it off until mid-afternoon, and be back to work at five o'clock in the afternoon for the next round.

The other bartenders and I had a unique relationship; I was the only woman there when I started, so I was to be protected while behind the bar. The bouncer, the owner, and the other bartenders treated me like a little sister and became my family. We even spent holidays together at the bar, like orphans on Christmas Eve, toasting our good fortune to have each other. This lifestyle afforded me the luxury of completely shelving many of my symptoms. I now rotated among four states of being: energized and manic behind the bar, drunk, sleeping, or hung over. There was no extra brain capacity to allow the obsessive thoughts to creep in and take hold; if they did, they would soon enough be anesthetized.

The alcohol masked both my manic highs and my suicidal lows because I simply could no longer see them; in my head, all the craziness ran together and lines of emotional distinction often blurred. It did no such masking to the outside world, however. My mood swings and anxiety were such that one of my bouncer bodyguards nicknamed me "Sybil," after the novel about a woman with multiple personalities, and never tired of asking, "And who are we today?" when I came to work. His other favorite thing to do was to point out the broom in the corner, turn to me and say, "Nice park job." Evidently my bad moods were . . . bad.

One night at closing time, I was invited to breakfast by a man whom I'd been watching for several months. He was a player; everyone knew him, everyone loved him, and he always seemed to have a ton of cash and a ton of friends around him. He was a good ten years older than I was, which, of course, made him even more attractive. Also, he had just moved upstairs from the apartment I shared with two girlfriends, and so I figured I had geography in my favor. I accepted his invitation.

We hung out most of that night and again the next. There was no denying the attraction, but there was a lot of denying pretty much anything else; we had nothing in common. He was blue-collar all the way, representing the life I wanted, eventually, to transcend: He worked the three-to-eleven shift at an automobile manufacturing plant, had no college degree, and had no aspirations beyond clocking out after his shift and getting high. I was a princess to him; oh, sure, I was a bartender at the time, but he could see I was destined for great things. I was, after all, going to be a real writer someday.

Despite the lack of common interests, our relationship flourished. He made me feel safe and loved for reasons that were never quite clear. Nothing mattered to him except where his next beer or joint was coming from—and being with me. We took trips to beaches and sat in hot tubs drinking wine. Every girl wanted to be with him, and he was with me. We moved in together after a year.

It was my first time living with a man, and for the first time in a long time, I felt like I belonged. True, he was a staggering drunk most of the time, but he was such a lovable drunk that I didn't even care. On our first Christmas together, he gave me a black-and-white pearl ring; six months later, half in the bag while shopping one day, he bought me the tiniest diamond ring ever made from the jewelry counter at T.J. Maxx. I was thrilled. I was engaged.

He was an hourly worker at the auto plant and always volunteered for layoffs or out-of-state training sessions, any excuse to party more than he already did. The drama in our relationship often mirrored the drama of my childhood, and I often thought I was simply destined for that kind of life. But I was always able to look past the frustration and anger; after all, the worst he did was drink and smoke pot—none of the really bad stuff—and, again, he was so darn lovable when he was loaded that he was just irresistible.

The boyfriend bought me a golden retriever puppy for Christmas one year. I was trying to paper-train him by gating him in the kitchen while we were out, and we came home one night to find the kitchen in complete disarray: shredded newspaper everywhere, with poop and pee mixed throughout. A novice dog-owner, and still harboring the paralyzing fear of what would happen if someone got mad at me—the boyfriend or the landlord—I told the boyfriend to take the dog outside as I got down on my hands and knees to clean up.

An hour later, the two of them had not returned. The car was still in the driveway, so I knew that they had walked wherever they had gone. Since two of the boyfriend's favorite haunts were a few blocks down the street, I figured I knew where to start looking, and I didn't have to look any further than the first dive.

I walked in and there he was, standing in a bar with my dog in his arms, using him to pick up a girl. I walked up to the three of them, took the dog, and went home. The boyfriend followed, about three hours later. I swore and cried all the way home but never said a word to him about it because, of course, he'd get mad, which I couldn't bear.

Right around that time, I realized I needed to get out of the bartending scene. I was smart, college-educated, and ready for something new. I found a job as a legal secretary for a one-man downtown law office. The boyfriend bought me a briefcase and a dozen roses my first day. He was proud of me, and he showed it. He made me breakfast and made sure I had lunch money and the car had gas. Suddenly, I was Melanie Griffith in *Working Girl* and he was my Harrison Ford.

On disability from the plant—his doctor was always game to provide excuses for him, as long as he was paid in cash—the two of us would meet at happy hours after I finished work and then grab dinner somewhere. I was, in retrospect, amazingly successful at not getting drunk during the week because I didn't want to show up at work with a hangover; unfortunately, when the weekends rolled around, I was more than ready to make up for lost time.

ON HALLOWEEN THAT YEAR, I LEARNED MY FRIEND'S FIANCÉ HAD TESTICULAR CANCER.

The two of them were former roommates of mine, and we had all lived together before I moved in with the boyfriend. My friend's fiancé was a regular at my bar, and was one of the few guys down there who could verbally spar with me and have a chance at sometimes winning. He earned my grudging respect, and when I saw how much he loved my friend, he earned my friendship. He was like a brother to me while we were roommates, and his illness was devastating.

The boyfriend was not as affected, or, if he was, he showed his grief by disappearing for days at a time and showing up with a hangover and someone's lipstick on his shirt. I couldn't be bothered with it at the time, but it was the beginning of a long, drawn-out end for us. As we started pulling apart, he—in truth, we—became at times angry, repentant, hopeful, frustrated, defeated, and simply tired. I began to confide in my family about his philandering, alluding to his drug use, and for the most part I was met with sympathy and encouragement. They already all disapproved of him because of his drinking.

I had been corresponding with my uncle during this time, and shortly after Thanksgiving, my mother, younger brother, and I went to visit him in New York; despite my parents' offer he'd decided to stay in his own home. He had started showing the telltale bruises and welts of full-blown AIDS, and had lost a lot of weight from his already thin frame. He was nervous about going out because gay-bashers were making sport of beating up AIDS-afflicted men walking the streets, and the few times we managed it, it took some convincing to get him out of the apartment for some fresh air.

During the visit, we were all trying to make conversation, small talk, whatever, trying to avoid the obvious discussion of: what does it feel like to know you're dying? I started telling him a "my boyfriend did another mean thing" story, when suddenly my uncle just snapped.

"Why are you even with that asshole? If he treats you bad, leave him. Don't complain about it for the rest of your life. Just leave and get it over with!" He got up and left the room, he was so frustrated.

I was mute with shock. My uncle had never spoken to me—or anyone, as far as I knew—this way in my life. I was offended, hurt, and embarrassed, and probably did not speak directly to him for the rest of the visit. It took months for the sting to wear off and understanding to set in, but by then it didn't matter; I wouldn't see him again before he died.

My friend's fiancé went through surgery and several rounds of chemo over the next couple of months, but the cancer wasn't going away. We had an event at the bar to raise money for him to travel to another state for some experimental treatment, but that didn't help him either. When he started dying, we took turns being with him at the hospital. His family and girlfriend had pretty much been camping out in the waiting area; there were sleeping bags, pillows, blankets, and various toiletries strewn about like he was the only sick person in the ward. But that's how we felt because he was so young.

The day he died, we were all standing around him, my friend and his mom holding his hands, the rest of us just touching whatever part of him we could reach. I was holding his left foot and all I remember is thinking, *God, this foot is so swollen. Can't they do anything about that?* And then he was dead. He was twenty-six.

He died in February. My uncle died two months later.

IN JUNE OF THAT YEAR, THE BOYFRIEND CAME TO THE OFFICE WHERE I WAS WORKING.

I'd moved up a bit in the legal world, size-wise, taking a job at a larger firm and taking on more responsibility. I was starting to feel more comfortable in the suit world and was seriously thinking about moving out and getting a place of my own. I spent many hours commiserating with another woman in the office about the transgressions of our respective men, the conversations always ending with the same conclusion. We needed to leave them.

The day he came to the office changed everything. He wore a look I'd never seen before. He wasn't smug, he wasn't cocky, he wasn't putting on his "I don't give a damn" mask. He looked . . . crushed, somehow. He asked if we could take a walk, and, even though it was too early for lunch, I could tell it was important and said yes.

We went to a nearby park and sat on a bench, and he turned to me, his face ashen. "I'm HIV-positive," he said.

It felt like a curtain fell on the part of my brain that had housed my life up until that moment. Nothing would ever be the same.

We were trapped together in an unspoken pact of silence because this was not something people could know. As I'd already known from the experience with my uncle, there was no treatment, nothing to prevent the inevitable. He made me promise not to tell anyone, and as sad and destroyed as he looked, I knew I could never leave him now. I couldn't leave a dying man. I had to take care of him.

After a while he said, "You should probably get tested."

Once again I was stunned; it hadn't even occurred to me that he could have given it to me.

"You probably don't have it, but they said I should bring you down for a blood test." And what struck me was not what he said as much as how he said it. It was almost as if he didn't care if I had it. It was all about him; I was an afterthought. But I let him lead me to the Red Cross building around the corner, allowed my blood to be drawn, digested the directive at the time that I would never be able to give blood again because I'd had sexual relations with an HIV-positive partner, and went home. I had to wait for two weeks before I would know anything.

And even then, even if the test was negative, I had to be retested in three months and then again in six because the virus can appear up to six months after exposure. So, I thought, *What I really need to do is find a way to sleep for half a year because I will not be able to function with this hanging over my head; even without OCD, I'd be paralyzed.* But there was no way to do that. I still had to go to work and talk to people and schedule hearings and closings and go on living. I compartmentalized this part of my life so that the others parts could go on, which, in retrospect, was one of the greater feats of managing a mental illness. And, of course, I could not tell a soul because that would be embarrassing to him—one more secret for me to carry, but, at least this time, it wasn't mine.

I then accomplished another in a long list of quite remarkable reframings. Instead of feeling sorry for myself, I took on a caregiver role. My mindset was simple: My boyfriend is going to die, it will be a long, slow, agonizing death, and I will be with him every step of the way. I will not abandon him, now or ever. I will learn to trust him again because he will have no choice but to be faithful this time. This disease will make him love only me, and we will be happy together till death do us part, in nine or ten years.

And I somehow convinced myself that I was okay with this.

My first blood test was negative. I sobbed with relief, and was reminded to return in three months. My second blood test was negative, and I sobbed with relief and promised to come again in three more months. My third blood test was negative, and they said I didn't have to come back anymore. This was a little easier said than done; the thought was already at an obsessive level. I couldn't just turn it off.

My fourth, fifth, sixth, seventh, and eighth blood tests were negative.

Through all of this, the boyfriend rebounded in spirit and energy and, incredibly, wanted to have unprotected sex with me. His extreme lack of remorse and accountability started to sink in at this point. He still would not tell me how he thought he might have come by this particular virus; in fact, counting on my allegiance and, presumably, stupidity, he suggested he may have picked it up some five or six years ago and it had only now shown up.

I knew this could not be the case, however, for two reasons: HIV shows up in the blood within six months of exposure, and he gave blood through work every year. If I'd been with him at that point for almost three years, then it was pretty much a certainty that he was exposed during our relationship. And he did not do IV drugs; this much I knew. He did not like needles in any way, shape, or form, although for the first time, I almost wished he had.

Through all of this, I'd developed a habit of calling my two older brothers in the middle of the night after having way too much to drink. I depended on their support and would cry on their shoulders for hours, although never revealing the HIV angle. One night, in the midst of my sobs, I asked my oldest brother, "Why does God keep doing this to me?" He thought about it for a minute and said, "Because you're not learning." His wisdom annoyed me.

I'D ONCE AGAIN TRAPPED MYSELF IN A WELL-WORN CLOAK OF SHAME AND GUILT AND FEAR.

Playing Florence Nightingale was burying me, but, although strangely energized by this secret, I couldn't talk to anyone about it, not even the boyfriend. He went about his life as if he'd only had a cold that was now gone. He was partying and living the same life he'd lived before, and I became even more confused. Here I was, wanting—needing—to take care of him, to give up my own life to make his final days better, and he was acting like nothing had happened. I was lonely and angry and no longer feeling any of the love or belonging or sense of being needed that I had once felt.

And then one day, I met a lawyer about fifteen years my senior who was friends with my boss at the law firm. He took an unusual interest in me, which I, at first, mistook for the usual romantic interest. But that was not the case. He just thought I was a nice kid who needed a little cleaning up, a little direction, a little guidance.

Without the boyfriend's knowledge, which was easy to manage because he was back to working the second shift and partying with his buddies for hours afterward, my new friend began trying to polish me up a little. He suggested that the miniskirts and tight blouses might be inappropriate for a law office, and showed me where to shop for *nice* clothes: the kind that didn't say "stretch" anywhere on the label. Over time he helped me develop a professional wardrobe, and he would often take me to lunch at nice restaurants and talk to me about life and the future and why there are two forks next to the plate.

To the outside world, it would seem we were having an affair, and he didn't care. He knew we weren't, and he proudly introduced me to people we ran into on the street or at restaurants. We played golf and had lunch and did things that people do who are really friends. I can't imagine it didn't initially cause some discord in his marriage, but, if it did, he never mentioned it. In fact, I envied his wife and how lovingly he spoke of her.

He cared about me, and that's all there was to it, so it bothered him no end that I was living with the boyfriend. I jokingly told him to join the club, but he didn't smile. The bad news is, after all his efforts, he would be one day soon bailing me out of the suicide ward at a local hospital. The good news is he was all smiles at my wedding almost a decade later.

As time went on, and the boyfriend showed no signs of wanting to survive his diagnosis, my anxiety blossomed. Suddenly, there was not enough hair on my body to pluck out, not enough acne to pick at. And a new obsession had begun to manifest: denying myself food. I was out of control emotionally, and so I starved myself physically. It gave me a sense of control. It started out innocuously; the boyfriend had agreed to start eating better to keep his immune system healthy, and so I started eating healthy, too. When I lost a few pounds, I thought, *Hey—this is pretty neat.* I'd forgotten what it felt like to lose weight.

I ate less and less because the thrill of getting on the scale and seeing the numbers go lower and lower was addictive. A little taller than average, I wasn't heavy to begin with, maybe 140 pounds, but by the end of that year I'd lost thirty pounds. Also by the end of that year, I'd decided I did not want to watch the boyfriend kill himself more quickly by drinking and smoking pot, and I remembered that I'd thought of leaving him long before his blood test results. With the help of a friend who had been waiting impatiently for me to get my proverbial shit together, I found my own place, took off the ring, and left the boyfriend, presumably to die alone.

CHAPTER EIGHT

RED BELT

"RED CAN BE SEEN AS A SYMBOL OF THE POWER OF THE RED-HOT SUN. A RED-BELT STUDENT MUST LEARN TO PRACTICE CAUTION AND CONTROL IN THE USE OF HIS ABILITIES."

~GWEN BRUNO, LIVESTRONG.COM

At red belt, we were required to start teaching during class. The instructor would separate out the students by level and assign different red belts to teach groups of lower levels. We were also required to start performing in "demos": pre-belt-graduation shows designed to pump up the audience and create some energy among those graduating to their next belt.

After teaching a certain number of hours and performing in a certain number of demos, we achieved the coveted red *gi*,—short for *karategi* or karate training uniform—worn only by those who earned it. Having never taught nor performed in front of an audience, and having no desire to ever do so, these were not easy tasks for me.

New things are not always easy. But they're often necessary for growth.

1989, AGE TWENTY-SEVEN.

As I pull into the driveway for one of my prodigal visits, my father stands outside on the little slab of cement we call a patio, firing up the gas grill for dinner. He has a beer in his hand and a backup on the picnic table.

I say hello, head inside, and make myself at home, which includes verbally jousting with the little brother and sister I barely know; regaling my mother with stories of my new job, new boss, and new life without the boyfriend; and generally acting the part of the perfect daughter I want to be. Actually, what I really want to be is twelve again and to try to do things right this time, but, of course, I can't; even if I had a time machine, it wouldn't have gotten rid of the rituals and compulsions. This is the trouble with always wanting to start over: I don't know what is wrong in the first place, and so I can't make things right on the next try. It is a cycle of failure.

After dinner, I talk my mother into heading to the bar down the street to have a few drinks and catch up a bit on each other's lives. My old watering hole is now a respectable restaurant, and we are able to sit and talk for two or three hours. It is absolutely lovely, visiting with her in this way. And because of my non-eating, after just a couple of glasses of wine, I am blasted.

We return home after midnight to find my father in one of his dark moods, my little brother barricaded up in his attic bedroom, and my little sister cowering in bed, fully clothed, with the covers pulled up to her chin. When my brother hears us come in, he bolts down the attic stairs and turns on me.

"Why do you even bother coming home?" he screams at me through tears. "This happens every time! And then you leave! And we're stuck here! Why do you even bother?"

Standing there, watching this boy's heart break before my eyes, I lose it. I'd had just enough to drink to be belligerent and self-righteous;

I tell my mom, brother, and sister to get some clothes, and I make them come home with me. I have one child in my car and my mother has one in hers, behind me. We drive three hours on the thruway at two in the morning. I, of course, am drunk.

When I awake the next morning, I am horrified at what I've done—not that I've kidnapped my family, necessarily, but that I endangered their lives with my drunken anger. But once that self-flagellation evaporates, I am able to do what I've wanted to do for years and never had the courage to.

I write my dad a letter, asking him to quit drinking. I tell him that I know how hard it is, and how frightening, and how unfair, because I am an alcoholic as well. But it is time; he is losing his family. It is a heartfelt plea for him to stop from someone who understands. I tell him I have to quit, too, and how hard it is for me.

My mom takes my brother and sister home the next day, and my mom says my dad crumpled up my letter and threw it in the garbage. He quit drinking, though, which was somewhat ironic because I didn't.

I HAD TAKEN A JOB AT YET ANOTHER, LARGER LAW FIRM.

Already on the decline toward my own inevitable rock bottom, my new boss couldn't have been better suited for me. He was high-strung, controlling, and somewhat paranoid. He also was very demanding, very scattered, very disorganized, and very manic, thinking nothing of cancelling a ten-attorney deposition that had taken weeks to coordinate and schedule simply because he was feeling overwhelmed. He often reminded me of an alcoholic without the alcohol, and I was the classic codependent counterpart.

Despite all of the drama, he was very kind to me—parental even. The paradox made working for him particularly challenging, and also made it so much easier to starve myself; anxiety thrives on that kind of emotional conflict. This time period was when I first heard the phrase "I'll show you; I'll hurt me" to describe how women tend to turn their anger inward. And I did, I did, I did. I starved myself until my upper arms looked like swizzle sticks, and then I starved some more. It was as if working for this man gave me permission to punish myself—as if I needed a reason, and here it was.

People began to comment on my weight loss, and not always positively. But ask any anorexic; when it comes to weight loss, even an insult is a compliment. There simply is no such thing as too thin. Eventually, my firm sent me to an eating disorder clinic where I spent four sessions being essentially ridiculed by a man for being stupid: "You know you're hurting your body, right? And that this is just a cry for attention?" Maybe he thought he could appeal to the intellectual side of me, the side that got good grades and loved law. But, if that's the case, then he wasn't a very good counselor. He just made me angry, and when I get angry— well, we already know what happens: "I'll show you . . . ."

I started seeing another counselor instead, a young woman who specialized in alcoholism. I went to group therapy twice a week but continued to drink, figuring that, as long as I was getting help for it, I was headed in the right direction. I was hoping that maybe I wouldn't have to quit at all, that somehow she could teach me to keep it under control, and then maybe I could have the self-medication without the self-hate. I never mentioned the other issues: the hair-pulling and skin-picking and obsessive thoughts about whatever they were about that day; it didn't occur to me that these issues were anything other than my own personal demons.

The irony was that because of those demons, even if I didn't self-medicate, I would continue to self-hate.

IT WAS BECOMING MORE AND MORE OBVIOUS TO OTHERS THAT I HAD SOME SERIOUS ISSUES.

As the months wore on at the law firm, I'd developed an unidentifiable skin rash on my legs that mimicked psoriasis, my hair was thinning even where I wasn't plucking, and I was picking at my face until it bled, sometimes while at my desk.

And while many of us went out for drinks after work with some frequency, my drinking was different. Even if no one else knew it, I knew it. And God, did it make me angry—why I had to feel like an out-of-control freak, judged and dismissed, or worse, judged and taken advantage of for doing the exact same thing that everyone else was doing: having a couple of glasses of wine with friends. And often, like "gaydar," addicts can recognize each other; another woman at the firm knew my secret as well. She was a paralegal and a recovering alcoholic. She asked me on occasion if I would like to join her at her twelve-step fellowship meeting, to which I would kindly reply, "No, thank you; I've got this." Then I would walk away fuming with an indignity I would never share with her because I didn't want to make her mad.

The most visible symptom of the downward spiral was still the weight loss, and eventually my boss convinced me—by threatening my job, if I recall correctly—to go to my regular doctor, whom I'd previously seen on several occasions with the imagined brain tumors, cancers, and rare diseases I was always convinced I had. As I waited in the exam room for him, I stepped on the scale and it read 100 pounds. I stepped off and sucked in my gut some more and got back on: ninety-nine pounds. Off again, on again—I was determined to keep it at ninety-nine. That's how the doctor found me when he returned: stepping off and on the scale.

Finally, at long last, he truly thought something was wrong with me. He gave me a stern talking-to about the dangers of starving myself, a prescription for an anti-anxiety drug called Ativan, and an appointment for the following week. I was no longer crazy, imagining things that were wrong with me; this eating disorder thing really did exist. I vowed then and there to sustain the anorexia because it gave me a tangible, identifiable explanation for some of what was going on in my head.

Also right around that time, I'd been hanging out at a very boutique-y bar where only the coolest people hung. I was getting quite confident with my social butterfly persona: the "fake it till you make it" Maggie. I always arrived after work, professionally attired. I had my first glass of wine to unwind and shake off the day, and then my night started. I usually ended up by myself those nights because the more I drank, the meaner I got—heck, *I* didn't even want to go home with me half the time—but there was one man I had a crush on who was starting to pay attention.

He was older, distinguished, and wealthy. He drove a nice car, had a terrific career, and was very handsome; in short, he was everything I wanted in a man. Here was a man who could save me, who could give me my happily ever after. This was it, I told myself; this is where I start over. We flirted for weeks, and finally one night he said, "Come on; let's get out of here. Let's go dancing."

We went to a local hotel restaurant that boasted a popular dance floor. After checking our coats, we danced the night away—and I drank the night away as well. When it came time to leave, I could not for the life of me find my coat check marker, and I vaguely recall making a very big deal about this with the coat check girl. I am nothing if not dramatic—and combative—when I'm loaded. My vague recollection includes a very clear scene. Somehow, eventually, I left with my coat.

This man and I agreed that I would follow him home from the hotel. We each got in our cars, he pulled out, and I pulled out after him. I drove down the highway for many, many miles, swerving and weaving in my drunken stupor, before realizing I had no idea what his car looked like anymore or if I was even still in the same state as him. I gathered enough of my wits together to get home in one piece and spent the rest of the night calling information, trying to find a man whose last name I couldn't remember.

The next time I saw him, I coolly approached him with the coat check marker I'd eventually found in one of my pockets. "I believe this is yours," I said, with my best seductive voice.

He simply glared at me for a long moment, said, "Keep it," and turned his back. I'd never experienced such cruel, deserved, overt rejection, and the embarrassment and humiliation would have been unrecoverable had I not been heading down into an emotional abyss already. The experience served only to hasten the trip.

MY WEEKEND-LONG, TEN-YEAR HIGH SCHOOL REUNION WAS A THING OF BEAUTY.

It took place about a month after the Mr. Perfect fiasco and signaled the beginning of the end of my life as I knew it, although I couldn't see it at the time. What I saw was a very slender, sexy, successful, single young woman ready to go back and kick some high school ass. I had a T-top Nissan Pulsar, and now, thanks to my doctor, I had downers to mix with the booze. I also had a chip on my shoulder the size of Montana.

What I didn't have was any self-confidence, but that didn't stop me. After stopping to visit with my parents and dropping off my overnight bag, I got ready and headed out. I went into that reunion as if I owned the world, and that's what people saw. My makeup was perfectly applied to hide my facial scars, my eyebrows neatly penciled in. Zooming into the reunion parking lot with the T-top off the car, I made my entrance in a little black dress that clung to my skeletal frame like plastic wrap.

That is what I wanted them to see.

I didn't want them to see the train wreck that had become my life or to glimpse the truth: that facing the world alone evoked a daily struggle to get out of bed; that I was perpetually looking for someone to love me and make me feel safe, and perpetually failing because what I was looking for could never exist; that I often found that love and safety with married men because they could give me what I needed without asking anything in return; that I had just about run out of hope; and that I was a drunk and I pulled out my own hair and apologized for the rain. I did not want them to see that the harder I fell, the harder I needed to convince people I was on top.

I hung out with my few friends from high school, charmed them with my initial-drink smoothness, and got quietly-but-surely hammered. I flirted with boys that wouldn't give me the time of day in high school, made up dramatic stories about my current life and career that I knew couldn't be fact-checked, and eventually managed to get home each night. When it was all over, nursing a hangover and trying desperately to piece the weekend together in my head, I packed my bag and left my hometown. I drove the three hours back to my apartment and cried the whole way.

THANKSGIVINGS WERE A BIG EVENT IN MY FAMILY, BIGGER EVEN THAN CHRISTMAS.

Everyone came home for them if it was humanly possible; that was just how it was done. We gathered at various relatives' houses until we became too big to do so. Then we rented a cabin in the woods—a barn almost—on which we'd descend each year until, with marriages and kids, we no longer fit there either. The gathering then moved to a VFW, which had the added convenience of a stocked bar. We all tried our best to make it each year because we rarely saw our relatives anymore except for this one time of year. And I, at least, needed to show how much I'd grown or how successful I'd become or how happy I was. My Uncle Andy had always come home, too, and that was always the biggest thrill; Thanksgivings lost a certain amount of appeal after his passing.

In my head, I loved those Thanksgivings. In reality, they usually reverted to a scream-fest between my father and me, both of us inevitably spending the day slowly getting drunk. The occasions when he and I were wasted at the same time, in the same place, were few and far between, so we took advantage of these opportunities. I would lambaste him with every single thing he'd ever said and done to hurt me, and he'd do his best to ignore me, which would make me angrier still. From the time I was old enough to drive, which was also when I began to pick up, I ended these annual debates by driving away, drunk and angry, down two-lane country roads, and often in the snow.

The year of my high school reunion, with the pressure of my weight issues and anxiety-fueled drinking, I didn't want to go home for Thanksgiving. I'd never missed one, no matter what was going on in my life, but this year I guess I wasn't interested in being the show. It wasn't even lack of interest, really; I simply didn't have the energy. Trying to be someone I was not for the benefit of others was taking its toll; I was about as far down in the pit as I'd ever been, and, for the first time in my life, I didn't feel like crawling out.

My brothers in Boston would pick me up on their way home for holidays, and, as was our custom, they usually arrived at my place on the day before Thanksgiving. The evening before that, on Tuesday, I called my doctor's office to talk to my favorite nurse—the one who was trying to convince me that I didn't actually look good at ninety-nine pounds—and asked her about the anxiety medicine they'd put me on several months earlier.

Specifically, I asked what would happen if I swallowed the whole bottle.

The nurse asked me innumerable and often unrelated questions, which, I'm sure in hindsight, she was trained to do; within ten minutes, there was a knock on my door. I politely said, "Can you hang on? Someone's at the door." I opened it up and two uniformed police officers stepped in. One took the phone from my hand and told the nurse, "We've got her. We'll take it from here."

I silently cursed the nurse and made a mental note not to confide in her anymore.

One of them, who I decided was "Bad Cop," confiscated my bottle of pills; the other, who turned out to be "Worse Cop," just glared at me for several minutes until an ambulance arrived, whisking me away to a nearby hospital. I tried repeatedly to explain and convince everybody that I had simply been asking out of curiosity, and that I wasn't going to kill myself. They just nodded.

Once at the hospital, I repeatedly demanded my one phone call. "You're not under arrest," Bad Cop said. Clearly annoyed with me, he finally gave me a quarter for the pay phone and let me call my lawyer friend. His wife answered the phone, and sounded surprisingly calm for having received a 1:00 a.m. call from a crying woman asking for her husband. My friend, of course, had already told her about me, and I imagined her only surprise was how long it took for the phone call to come.

"Hi. Can you come and get me? I'm at the hospital," I told him. I was trying to sound both casual and brave—as brave as I could in a gown with my butt hanging out while crammed into a phone booth that I'm reasonably sure needed to be tested by the Centers for Disease Control. "There's been a big misunderstanding and I'd like to go home now."

My friend asked to speak to one of the cops, both of whom were hovering around the phone booth; I opened the door and handed the phone to Worse Cop, who was the closest. I only heard his end of the conversation and decided that I must have been the absolute worst thing he has ever seen in his career.

"Who's this?" he said, curtly. I couldn't hear the answer.

"What's your relationship to her?" he demanded. Again, I couldn't hear the answer.

"Look, your 'client' threatened to kill herself," he said. "She's not in police custody—she's in medical custody."

Yikes, I thought. *I did?* I thought I was just inquiring as to the physical ramification of ingesting more than the prescribed dosage of an anti-anxiety medication because maybe I was feeling a little anxious. As I listened to the one-sided conversation, I began to question my own motives. *Was* I trying to die? Was that what I was feeling when I made that phone call to the nurse? After all of these years, had I finally gotten to the point where suicide became a viable option?

And I knew the answer there was a resounding *yes*. And what kicked in next was pure panic.

"I'm sorry," I said, to the police, the orderly, anyone in the vicinity. "I'm sorry. I'm sorry. I'm sorry. I'm sorry. I'm sorry. I'm sorry. I'm *so* sorry."

While this litany of apologies continued in my head, my body was being transported to the state psychiatric facility down the street. The police told my lawyer friend he could pick me up there; I found out later he had to wait three hours before they would let him see me. In those three hours, I was evaluated by a bevy of psychiatrists and their students, telling each one that I was fine—really; I had merely been curious; I won't do it again, swear to God; and I really have to go now because my brothers will be at my apartment soon.

When at last I was released early the next morning, the attending physician pushed my wheelchair to the front door and offered a final piece of advice that I will cherish to this day: "Next time you do it, do it right." I couldn't understand why he was so angry with me. I said I was sorry.

When I finally made it back to my apartment, my brothers were waiting for me; my lawyer friend had left a semi-explanatory note for them on my apartment door while I was at the hospital. I was a physical wreck, having been verbally and emotionally battered much of the night with no sleep, but was quite shocked to see what an emotional wreck my oldest brother was. He was devastated.

I joined them on the sofa as my younger brother fetched me a cup of coffee. We sat in silence for several minutes, no one really knowing where to begin. Finally, my oldest brother asked, "What happened?" And, at last, I found the truth.

"I just didn't want to be here anymore," I said. "I just felt . . . done. That's all."

They mulled that over for a time, the two of them, not knowing what the heck to say, all of us pondering the shared portion of our lives from which I alone, I thought, did not emerge unscathed. When I next looked into the face of my oldest brother, I saw an anguish that nearly brought me to tears.

"Mag," he said, through his own tears, "Why?"

He was asking as if he honestly didn't know, and it was then I realized that maybe he was not unscathed after all. He'd obviously put at least some of it away in mental storage, judging by this question. He had no idea of the depths of my challenges, probably because I never once told him about them. They were shameful because they were secret—or was it the other way around? All he knew about was my alcoholism, and that was old news; he'd gone from listening to my dad's drunken nightly rants to listening to mine. It was life as we knew it. He didn't know the rest because nobody knew the rest.

"I'm just tired," I said. "Maybe I just didn't want to go home this time." It seemed as though it was only then that he remembered Thanksgiving was the following day, and some sort of understanding began to dawn on him.

Home.

Drinking.

Shouting.

Crying.

Leaving.

I mean, that's what it was all about, right?

THANKSGIVING THAT YEAR WAS CLOUDIER THAN MOST.
We decided we should still go and try to pretend everything was
normal and that I hadn't just spent the night in a mental hospital.
We all looked like hell but blamed it on the long trip and a poor
sleep. I didn't celebrate the holiday with my usual mixed drinks,
which probably was a stronger clue than anything that all was
not well. No one, however, asked what was wrong because no
one really wanted to know; we didn't get involved in each other's
issues. I got through the holiday, and my brothers brought me
back to my apartment the next day.

I was about as down as a person can be without actually being
prone. I zombied through work with no recollection of what I
was doing. Christmas was just ahead, my uncontested favorite
time of year, and I don't even remember if I got a tree. The
holiday came and went, and three days after Christmas I went to
a Friday happy hour at a downtown bar. I remember drinking a
couple of glasses of wine, which really wasn't a lot. Then again,
I probably hadn't eaten in a few days.

I left downtown and headed for my usual bar, and, as I veered
toward the off-ramp from one highway to another, I hit a patch
of ice and missed the curve. My car—my precious little Nissan
Pulsar—slammed head-on into a cement divider, completely
smashing in the front end. The hood flew up and the car bounced
back; I sat there, momentarily stunned, amazed, and slightly
pissed off that I was alive. I hadn't meant to hit the divider, I'm
reasonably sure, but, heck, as long as I had . . . oh, well. I put
my car in reverse, backed out onto the highway, pulled back into
traffic, edged over into the breakdown lane on the right, and
continued heading for my bar.

Within minutes, I was pulled over. The cop approached my
car, shone a flashlight in my window, and said, "What the hell
happened here?"

Although I tried to sound as coherent and business-like as I thought I looked, the totaled car I was driving was a dead giveaway. "Well, officer . . . well, I guess I missed a curve back there," I said. He told me to step out of the car and asked if I'd been drinking. I admitted to the two glasses of wine but said that I'd driven before having had much more alcohol and never hit anything, so that couldn't have been the problem; black ice was way more likely.

He examined the damage, called a tow truck, and asked where I wanted it towed. I probably answered a little too quickly—"Oh, take it to JB Auto; that's where it's always been fixed before!"— but I could tell by the way he was wrapping up the entire event that he was not going to ticket me, anyway. I sat in the back of the police car watching the tow truck pull away with my baby, and the cop said he would drive me home.

"Thank you," I said. "But I was on my way to my bar . . . can you drop me there?"

He looked at me, shook his head in disbelief, and started driving.

On the way, he said, "You know, I'm not going to arrest you for this, even though I should. I think you probably screwed up your life enough tonight, and I don't want to make it worse. But you shouldn't drink."

I thought about what he said, and answered, "You know, you're absolutely right. Hey! Can I do that breathalyzer thing, just for kicks?" He shook his head again and handed the device to me in the back seat. I blew almost twice the legal limit. *Hmm . . .* , I thought. *I guess I'm a little wasted after all.*

True to his word, the cop didn't arrest me for driving while intoxicated. He dropped me at the bar, and I went in and proceeded to drink myself into oblivion in the unconscious hope that I simply wouldn't remember the night.

When I woke up the next morning and pieced the previous evening together like a patchwork quilt, I knew I'd just defined and then hit "rock bottom." I called the paralegal from my law firm who'd been offering for years to take me to her fellowship meeting and asked her to pick me up. I never drank again. I was almost twenty-nine.

CHAPTER NINE

HIGH RED BELT

"THE RED BELT WITH BLACK STRIPE REPRESENTS 'FIRE AND HEAVEN.' IT SIGNIFIES HUMILITY, HONORS THE WISDOM, AND COMMITS TO THE WILLINGNESS OF BEING A LIFETIME STUDENT OF KENPO, WITH THE FINAL GOAL 'THE REAL HEAVEN.'"

~BRIGITTE SCHULTE AND MICHAEL MILLER,
CHINESEKARATEFEDERATION.COM

High red belt was the penultimate belt before first degree black belt in my Kenpo school. It was the stage at which we were invited to enter the black belt cycle: sixteen weeks of grueling four- to five-day-a-week classes and as many three- to five-mile runs;

three-mile runs had to be completed in twenty-four minutes to attain black belt.

The Saturday morning black belt candidate class was a three-hour cardio and material class. Every month on one of the Saturdays, candidates engaged in a black belt pre-test in which we were graded and assessed by the master of our school as to our readiness for black belt; if you were not deemed ready, you would be cut after a pre-test. The pressure was immense to complete the cycle.

———————————————⌒———————————————

1992, AGE THIRTY.

I'm sitting in my therapist's office, looking at him as though he just told me to walk into traffic. "I'm sorry. You want me to do what?" I ask him. I don't get too nervous because I've already decided I won't be coming back here.

"I want you to lie down on the floor, on your back, and kick this pillow," he says.

I look down at the pillow, then down at my legs. They are covered, from the knees down, with scabby, crusted sores that multiple dermatologists have diagnosed as probable psoriasis, but unlike any other psoriasis they've ever seen. There is no cure to offer me and only general remedies for the excruciating itching and the bleeding and scabbing that, because of the scratching, necessarily follow. Of course, for me, it's a double-edged sword; I want it to go away, but the scabs have reignited a part of my OCD that seems to be taking a firm hold.

From a purely cosmetic standpoint, I feel deformed. Some clod in the parking lot on the way into work one day asked if I'd been in a fire, and, of course, I said, "Yes," because that seemed as reasonable an explanation as any. I've been heading to the roof of the building on my lunch break every sunny day, stripping off my stockings, and letting my legs fry with the hope that the sun will cure them, but so far, no luck.

The other day, I read an ad from this therapist's office, indicating he specializes in "stress-related physical issues," and thought I might give it a shot. I've pretty much run out of dermatologists.

So here I am, lying on my back, frustrated to tears. He doesn't want to hear about the fact that quitting drinking has been challenging, or that I'm in graduate school for journalism and working full-time in a stressful law firm. He probably should hear about the fact that

I pluck out my eyebrows and eyelashes and pick at my skin until it bleeds, but it doesn't even occur to me to bring it up.

Instead, I lie here, kicking a pillow as though I'm pedaling a bike. It's supposed to force the negative energy from my body and, specifically, my legs, and release any pent-up aggressions and hostilities that may be causing my body to hurt itself. Personally, I feel quite stupid and embarrassed, but I keep kicking . . . and suddenly, I'm crying. Not just crying but sobbing. Kick, kick, kick, sob. When I finally can kick no more, I draw my legs up to my chest and lie there in a fetal position until normal breathing returns.

Maybe I'll come back after all.

A FEW NIGHTS AFTER MY LIFE-ALTERING CAR ACCIDENT, THE EX-BOYFRIEND CAME CALLING.

He wanted to spend New Year's Eve with me, still completely convinced I would come back—this, despite the fact that I'd been living in my own place for a year and a half. But the truth was that I still went back to the old place, and him, from time to time when I was weak and scared to be alone and wishing for everything that used to be but was no more. I kept a thread of the relationship alive because doing so ensured that I would not need to feel the underlying panic of disappointing him; that would trigger anxiety, which would trigger everything else, and I was trying so hard to cure myself of all of that once and for all.

Every now and then, I would give him a call and ask if I could stop over for a few minutes. I would walk into the flat, be instantly hit with the cloud of marijuana-laden air, and know I did the right thing by leaving him. But I'd usually also hang out for a while, just to feel that blanket of safety that he was somehow able to evoke.

Ironic, I know. The first man who ever made me feel safe and loved almost killed me.

He came over unannounced, which I hated. He was already wasted and he passed out on the couch; when he woke up a few hours later, I sat next to him there and told him that I couldn't drink anymore, and, in order to do that, I couldn't see him anymore. And that he had to leave. It was one of the most difficult conversations I'd ever had because leaving him was one of the hardest things I'd ever done. The concept of "the devil you know," suggesting that it's easier to stay in a less-than-ideal situation than to face the fear of an unknown future, is never more powerful than in an obsessive mind. Coupled with the realization that I was, without question, intentionally going to disappoint someone in this situation, the fact that we had been breaking up for a longer period of time than we were actually together makes perfect sense.

But leave he did. He went to another state to hang with his drug-running buddies for a few months, ostensibly to get over me. It was the best thing he could have done, really; cold turkey is always the best way for me, and my history would suggest that I wasn't capable of quitting him any other way. So he quit for me.

FOR SOMEONE WITH A DRINKING PROBLEM, QUITTING DRINKING IS NOT ALL THERE IS TO IT.

Addiction and the lifestyle associated with it are integral facets of our lives. They're not like a Monday night golf league that we can walk away from if we're too busy, but are more ingrained, like our families, our jobs, or our best friends. Quitting is like lopping off a part of yourself that was just as at home in your body as your right arm. There's a sense of loss, of grief, of anger, and of fear.

I was terrified. I thought I was the person that alcohol made me—funny, outrageous, vivacious, and engaging—and I thought I was going to lose all of those qualities by being sober. I was afraid I would be dull and lifeless and that my personality would go down the drain with the booze. Alcohol fueled my insanity; absent that insanity, what would I feel?

More importantly, I'd recently started writing professionally—for newspapers, magazines, any place that would buy what I wanted to put into words. And I always, always had a lot to say because I perceived my life as an interminable, drawn-out drama: a lengthy and ongoing suicide note to the world. Take away the alcohol, take away the drama created by it, and what would I have to write about? If I were no longer tragic, manic, depressed, drunk, hung over, panicked, or anxious, from where would my words come?

And it goes even deeper. For those of us a bit short of our self-esteem goals, the innate sense of failure with which we live is really quite nicely camouflaged by addiction. So is everything else that makes us so unhappy—in my case, OCD symptoms and the attendant anxiety. If you take away the drinking, those things don't necessarily go away with it; what, now, will mask them? The question then becomes, how else can we numb ourselves?

These were my thoughts as I sat on my couch—my cocoon—every day after quitting.

I got up for work earlier and earlier each day, eventually arriving at the office by 6:00 a.m. and staying until 5:00 p.m. I then went to my twelve-step meeting, at which I usually either cried or was silent for an hour, and then went home to my couch. Once settled in, I chain-smoked and listened to my mellow music: the sad songs that reminded me of "better" times—times, at least, when I knew what to expect every day and that, therefore, bestowed a level of comfort that evaded me on that couch. I eventually made my way to bed each night, and, like Sisyphus rolling the boulder up the mountain, I would start again the next day.

This went on for several months, and I could not understand why I felt so bleak. I did the two things I needed to do if I wanted to survive—I had quit drinking and left the boyfriend for good—and yet I still didn't feel like surviving. When exactly was that supposed to kick in? I had nothing to look forward to, nothing to do, and no one to do it with, anyway. Since I'd stopped hanging out at my bar, I had no friends except another young woman from my twelve-step meeting who helped me through the rougher patches by engaging me in movies and bowling and other activities I'd dismissed in the past as too tame. I was burning out and miserable at work—my boss was much more difficult to handle when my head was clear—and the only aspect of my life that seemed somehow controllable was my weight. Obsessing about what I ate was becoming a central part of each day.

It's hard to explain to someone without the obsession how gratifying it is to starve oneself. Try to imagine someone in the eye of a tornado with all of the elements of her life swirling out of control around her. The only thing that is calm and still in that storm is a plate of food. Now imagine that girl taking that plate of food and holding it, while the rest of her life swirls around her, and realizing that she controls that food. It does not control her. She can choose to eat it or not eat it. And if she chooses to not eat it, then she also controls her body. She maintains the calm in the eye of the storm. If she chooses to eat it, it swirls away and joins the chaos around her. She loses control. She loses the calm.

And so I didn't eat. I was able to go four, five days without eating solid food. Sometimes, I broke down and ordered a Pizza Hut pizza and ate the whole thing, but then I had to throw up, which

I knew I was capable of but could no longer stand to do. So I perfected the starving and allowed myself the occasional screw-up. It seemed to be a pretty even tradeoff. Quitting drinking made me feel as though I'd lost control of life as I knew it; by not eating, I'd latched onto the one thing I knew was still mine: my body.

Sometimes I would lie in bed, caress my hip bones, feel the concave of my stomach between them, count my ribs, and encircle my bicep with my thumb and forefinger—and I would think, *Yes, this is good. If I can do this, if I can just get down to skin and bones, rid my body of every ounce of fat, then maybe I can start over.*

I never got past that point, never tried to figure out exactly how I might start over—or what that might even mean—but lying there feeling all of my bones, I felt hope.

I attended twelve-step meetings during the week, and tried to make it through the weekends without killing myself because my home group only met Monday through Friday; weekend meetings would upset my established order of things, which was one of the elements of my life that was keeping me sane. One month into the program, I still wasn't leaving my couch except for work and meetings. Two months into the program, my older brother got married and I couldn't get myself together enough to attend; that is something I will regret forever, although I still believe there is nothing I could have done. I was not well physically, emotionally, mentally, or spiritually. And for a worthwhile wedding reception, you really need at least one of those.

I BEGAN SEEING THE PILLOW-KICKING PSYCHOLOGIST IN A LAST-DITCH EFFORT TO CURE THE RASH.

It had taken over my legs, since all of the dermatologists I'd seen were at a loss to explain it. I knew I was going through a rough period, even for me, and that stress could certainly be a factor. I met with him once or twice a week for months, and talked about all sorts of childhood issues and addiction issues—issues from the past. I never once, in all that time, mentioned that I compulsively picked at my face and pulled out my hair. I never brought it up because it didn't occur to me to bring it up.

Instead, I focused on the cultural phenomenon of the day: repressed memories of sexual abuse. People were popping up everywhere with success stories of unearthing such memories in therapy. I became convinced that this, finally, would be the answer to my lifelong mental issues—that this was the only reasonable explanation for my feelings about myself and for my need to sublimate my anxiety into physical attacks on my own face and body. I simply must have been sexually abused as a child, and all I had to do was remember by whom and I would be cured.

I spent weeks on this mission, trying to regress and force an epiphany that would fix my life. The shrink went through the list of usual suspects: my father, who never laid a hand on me except when it was wrapped around the occasional hairbrush, and uncles, babysitters, and older neighbors, none of which triggered any memories. I was getting more frustrated by the week, and I didn't understand it. I had to have been molested. It would explain everything. So what if I have absolutely no recollection of it; it's the only thing that makes sense.

Then I started thinking about a family friend named George. He was my dad's best friend and just a nice, nice guy who tried to help my dad and my family through some of the tougher times. He adored us and we adored him, and he always signed his birthday cards "Georgie Porgie." One day, he was supposed to come over and didn't come, and, after receiving no answer on the phone, my dad went to his house to see what was wrong.

The house was locked and the garage door closed; my dad, thinking maybe George had just forgotten and made other plans, came home.

It turned out George was in the garage the whole time, with a hose leading from his muffler into his car window.

George's suicide devastated my father, and I'm sure we were sad, too, although we were probably too young to understand. As an adult, however, I grabbed onto that suicide as the Holy Grail for which I'd been searching: George must have molested me and killed himself out of guilt. It all fit so neatly. I was cured.

Except, of course, I wasn't—for several reasons, not the least of which was because George never touched me. I wasn't molested. There was, at the time, no simple cause for the way I felt about myself, and therefore no simple cure. My "afflictions"—being a drunk and pulling out my eyelashes, among others—were certainly a driving force, but I hadn't yet identified the blanket of shame that perversely comforted me each day. In any event, I decided from this experience that I probably had enough demons in my own head to last a lifetime, and maybe I should stop looking for outsiders.

I allowed the psychologist to work his magic in helping me rid my body of whatever stress was causing the leg rash and then stopped treatment. In my mind, it was done. There was nothing left to talk about.

After about three months sober, I began to see a proverbial light at the end of the tunnel. Actually, what I saw was a light at the top of what I envisioned as the dark pit in which I existed; I felt myself begin to crawl out, ever so slowly—but wanting, finally, to find the top, to see what was up there and out there for me. I saw vague glimpses of me wanting to live again.

IT BECAME APPARENT THAT I HAD TO GET MY LIFE BACK IF I WANTED TO SURVIVE.

I applied to graduate school to study journalism, took my Graduate Record Exams, got loans, and started school eight months after I quit drinking. I was working full-time at the law firm and attending classes. When I realized I was headed toward mental burnout, I went back to what I knew would re-energize me: tending bar. Foolhardy though it may have seemed, tending bar gave me a sense of confidence, and therefore a positive energy, that no other job had managed to provide. I stayed sober, earned the extra money I needed for school, and also got the energy boost I needed so desperately.

On the other hand, between classes, the law firm, tending bar, and my twelve-step meetings, I was running on empty. It would seem I simply traded obsessions. And I was about to do it yet again.

My law firm's annual Christmas party that year was on a Friday night at a local restaurant, one I hadn't been to before. Situated between the restaurant and the parking lot was a karate studio; I glanced in as I passed by and was instantly transfixed. Something about what they were doing in there grabbed me by the soul— that's the only way I can explain it. I'd never done anything physical in my life, had never played organized sports save for a year on the bench of the JV girl's basketball team, and was loathe to step out of my rigid routine, particularly alone. But the next morning, a Saturday, I went back to that place, walked in by myself, and joined.

Joining the karate class signaled the beginning of the end of my twelve-step program days. My favorite meeting conflicted with my karate schedule, and, rather than choosing another meeting that would accommodate me, I chose to substitute karate. Karate took care of both the mental and physical issues from which I was overtly suffering, serving the dual purpose of keeping me away from happy hours and forcing me to eat well or risk passing out in class from the exertion. Fortunately, I've always been keenly competitive and am satisfied with nothing less than my best, and, with karate, that meant maintaining my nutrition and energy. My need to win beat out my need to starve, most likely saving my life in the process.

I threw myself into karate as I threw myself into anything else: obsessively. It was the perfect place for me. I was actually encouraged to push myself until it hurt, encouraged to punch and be punched, kick and be kicked. Ostensibly, the goal was to become so proficient at the martial arts that we would never actually have to use them—but working toward that goal? Pure pain; I loved every minute of it. I worked out four to five days a week, rising quickly through the belts.

The only problems I continuously struggled with were the skin and eyebrows; I was still picking and plucking, and, because I have historically sweat like a man, I had to be very careful about my makeup sweating off during class. I kept an eyebrow pencil handy in the locker room and found opportunities to sneak in and touch up every chance I got. Oddly enough, that, to me, was the problem. Not that I had open sores all over my face or no visible eyebrows, but that I couldn't keep them camouflaged in karate. That fact alone should have been enough to compel me to research these behaviors; that I was still unable to stop doing them even after I entered recovery for alcoholism was more frustrating than I could have imagined. But I didn't research them. It still did not occur to me that they were quantifiable, recognized behaviors—of OCD or anything else. I thought they were simply mine.

After finishing graduate school, I moved to a little apartment near the karate *dojo* that harbored no ghosts of lives past, ex-boyfriends, or traumatic life events. My writing was coming along as I covered board meetings and local events for a weekly newspaper, and it seemed for all intents and purposes that I was finally beginning to live the life of a relatively normal, sane person. Oh, sure, I smoked a pack of cigarettes a day, wore cake makeup in a failed effort to conceal the damage I was doing to my face, and I still would not swim for fear my penciled-in eyebrows would wash off, but all in all, life was good. I'd been sober a couple of years and was looking ahead and seeing light.

I MET MY HUSBAND IN THE PARKING LOT OF THE KARATE STUDIO.

He'd seen me in class before because his class followed mine, and he waited on the sidelines for his to start, but I hadn't seen him until that day. We were cutting through the parking lot of our karate studio to get to the Corporate Challenge, an annual charity 5K run that began in the park behind the karate studio, and he caught up to me and introduced himself.

We flirted a bit on our walk to the Challenge, and I remember thinking that he was handsome and obviously successful, and, therefore, clearly out of my league. But he called me for lunch, and I was hooked. Our early dating days had some tense moments, complicated immediately by the fact that it was bad form to date a lower belt, but if I'd learned nothing else in recent years, it was to go after what I wanted.

At some point, I gave him the Cliffs Notes version of my complicated past, and he liked me anyway. I saw in him a chance for a normal life, the kind of future I'd imagined, with kids, dogs, maybe a mortgage along the way. Having now been sober for three years, there had been a gradual shift in my expectations and needs in a relationship that I hadn't even been aware was occurring. This was a different kind of relationship for me—not necessarily based on the "safe and loved" requirement as much as on a "Will we be able to talk over breakfast in fifty years?" condition. And I decided we could.

Though we had our differences and scary moments like any other couple, one day I began to realize that we were having many moments that weren't so much like any other couple; I was sabotaging the relationship with my craziness. It seemed that even though I'd gotten sober, my moods and anxiety had not, as I'd anticipated, dissolved with the liquor. In fact, they were becoming more pronounced as time went on.

I also started suffering from anxiety attacks, which I'd probably had all along but were masked by the depressive qualities of alcohol. They were mild at first, meaning no one noticed but me, but, one day, people noticed. My boyfriend and I attended a publicity event for a national motorcycle daredevil and were invited into the trailer where the promotional crew was lounging. I didn't know anybody except my boyfriend and his friend, who'd invited us to the event, and the trailer was crowded. Suddenly, I became so claustrophobic that I couldn't breathe. It felt as if my lungs were going to burst right out of my chest if I did not get out of there immediately. And I fled.

I got out into the air and started to settle down a little; I was no longer hyperventilating. Tears were streaming down my face, although I didn't remember wanting to cry, and when the first few people came out to check on me, they were concerned I was having a heart attack. When my boyfriend made his way out to me, he tried to understand what had happened but didn't, really. I told him we needed to leave immediately.

Soon I was having similar attacks when forced to wait in line too long at the grocery store, or at a party when a specific end time had not been set in advance, or being made to wait in a doctor's office. I would start to feel panicky and claustrophobic, and, wherever I was when the attack hit, I had to get out. The attacks would send me spiraling into a low period, once again fueling the anxiety, which once again fueled the compulsive rituals.

While I believed I was doing some of my best writing through all of this, I also realized it probably wasn't healthy to rely on panic for inspiration. Suffering variously between these intense mood swings and full-blown anxiety attacks, I knew that any hope of a "normal" relationship was fading fast.

While my highs and lows were a challenge for my boyfriend, they were more so for me, and sometimes the extremes took their toll emotionally. I often spent days at a time in bed, too depressed to move. It never occurred to me, despite my usual affinity for all things medical, to consult a physician about this. This was not physical. This was mental, and, even with my history of hypochondria, this didn't count. After the particularly frightening anxiety attack at the publicity event, however, I decided enough was enough and went to the doctor.

"It's like this, doc," I said. "I can actually stand back and watch the needle on my mood-o-meter go up and down. Seriously. I can intellectually watch my emotions skyrocket and plummet with no discernible rhyme or reason. I can feel the walls closing in, feel my lungs closing up, and I can't control it. All I can do is sit back and watch and hope I don't do something immeasurably stupid while it's happening. What's going on here?"

My doctor, who I inexplicably still adored despite his earlier advice for my anorexia—"Relax. It will go away."—replied, without so much as shining a light in my eyes, "It's just PMS. Learn to live with it." He may as well have patted me on the head as he sent me, dumbfounded, on my way.

His nurse practitioner was in the exam room with us. After the doctor left, as I sat on the exam table sobbing in frustration, she put a prescription in my hand. "Take this," she said, almost conspiratorially. "It's an anti-anxiety medication called Zoloft. I think it'll help you. Call me in a month and we'll see where you're at; we may need to adjust the dosage to get it right." I took the prescription, hugged her, and knew I would not be coming back to this doctor.

I filled the prescription and immediately went home to do my Internet research on anti-depressants. From what I could gather, the goal was simply to shave off the extreme highs and extreme lows, kind of like a teacher dropping the aberrant test scores on a high school exam. What would remain would be a calm, likable, middle-of-the-road set of moods. I would be able to handle the everyday events and occurrences that had been my button-pushers in a more level-headed and logical way, e.g., no more threatening the lady ahead of me in the grocery store with bodily harm if she didn't get a move on.

It all sounded good on paper, but I was consumed, again, by a burning dilemma: If I take away my highs and lows, how will I write? How will I create? If I was worried about losing my personality when I quit drinking, I was even more concerned about losing it now. My words came from my conflict, my strife, my extremes, my highs, and my lows. Where would they come from if I took still more of them away?

And yet, if I didn't take the chance, I knew without question I would blow this relationship. There was a lot of baggage and history and issues about which I could do nothing, but this—the anxiety and the mood swings—was different; this was something I might be able to manage. I owed it to my boyfriend, and to myself, to give it a shot. I wanted to get married, have kids, play ball in the backyard, and hit some golf balls in my old age with my husband. I was thirty-three years old and ready to start my life. I started taking the pills.

At first, I didn't notice a difference. Gradually, however, I realized that I wasn't snapping at the littlest thing or suddenly euphoric over the price of tea. Things were just . . . normal. Calm. There were no crises; there was no need for any. I realized that if I'd found this wonder drug in middle school, my life would have been much, much different; but, then again, if I hadn't gone through what I went through, I wouldn't be where I am . . . or who I am.

Reintroducing myself in a gentler, saner form helped our relationship immensely. It's always reassuring to know your girlfriend's head won't spin completely around, "Exorcist-style," at, for example, a company dinner. I moved into my boyfriend's quaint stucco house on a tree-lined street in September. On moving day, as he cleaned the remaining vestiges of my existence from my apartment, I sat alone, sobbing on the front steps with my last little box of stuff. I knew that life as I had known it was over, and, though it was a good thing, it was also heartbreaking. I'd spent a lot of time and energy on the old, sick, unhappy me, and I'd developed a certain fondness for it. Once again, I was finding it painful to let go of the devil I knew; I actually grieved for its passing.

CHAPTER TEN

BLACK BELT

"THE BLACK BELT, THE ULTIMATE ACHIEVEMENT OF MARTIAL ARTS SKILLS, SYMBOLIZES THE 'DARKNESS BEYOND THE SUN,' EXPLAINS THE WORLD MARTIAL ARTS CENTER. EVEN AS HE TEACHES OTHERS, THE BLACK BELT HOLDER CONTINUES TO BROADEN HIS OWN UNDERSTANDING, CONTINUALLY SEEKING KNOWLEDGE AND ENLIGHTENMENT. WITHIN THE BLACK BELT LEVEL, A SEPARATE RANKING SYSTEM BREAKS DOWN MASTERY INTO DEGREES, OR LEVELS OF ACHIEVEMENT."

~GWEN BRUNO, LIVESTRONG.COM

The black belt cycle was similar to a four-month military boot camp. We attended our own classes, taught lower-belt classes, and ran several miles—all of them four to five times per week. It was total dedication. And through it all, the sense of utter, complete exhaustion after the Saturday-morning three-hour candidate class and run resulted in utter, complete self-satisfaction.

The high red belt and black belt cycles culminated in a three-day "power weekend," during which candidates were tested on *kata*, *kumite*, and everything in between, finishing with a seven-mile "fun run." If we passed power weekend, we achieved the rank of black belt.

The commitment and focus of the black belt cycle were unparalleled in my history; finishing power weekend was one of the proudest, sanest moments of my life. I developed a level of confidence and inner health that had until then eluded me. I tested myself, and I passed.

2012, AGE FIFTY.

"I thought you were just taking a group of girls skating," my husband said, trying to understand how this could have happened. "I didn't know you were skating, too."

"Yes, well, I've been skating for forty-five years," I said, "and I've never shattered my wrist. So I didn't plan on it."

We were in the emergency room, my wrist suspended from a barbaric device designed to straighten it out of its current "S" shape. The pain was excruciating, and I silently ranked it up there with childbirth; despite a lifetime of halfhearted attempts at hurting myself—of wishing, sometimes, for physical pain because it was more quantifiable than the pain in my head—I was surprised at how much I could hurt and still live.

I'd taken my tween daughter and her friends to a nearby ice rink for a fun Friday night out, something I'd done often when my children were younger. As they grew older, there weren't nearly the opportunities to spend time with them on weekends, and if spending time meant ice skating with a bunch of middle-schoolers, then I took what I could get. I helped the girls get skated up, got myself ready, and followed them out onto the ice where strobe lights were flashing and dance music playing. I watched them take off, arm in arm, got out on the ice myself, and promptly fell. I knew immediately that it was broken, even though I'd never broken a bone before. The pain was excruciating, and the "S" shape of the wrist within minutes confirmed my suspicion.

Once at the hospital, I was put in a room where the fracture could be "reduced," or straightened back out. It seemed like a very long time before the dripping medication began to make any sort of difference in the pain level, although it was hindered by my persistent need to vomit. My allergic reaction to narcotics does nothing to quell my desire for them when I'm feeling like this—though, in fact, I'd never felt this much agony without a baby being on the other side.

Suddenly, I began sweating profusely. The room started spinning and I knew I was going to faint; my blood pressure had dropped dangerously low. One nurse raised my feet so they were above my heart while another grabbed a cloth and started mopping the sweat that was pouring down my face and into my eyes. At one point, as medicated as I was, I saw a strange look on her face and realized that she had just mopped off my eyebrows, which were penciled in daily with Revlon Color-Stay Brow Liner and Brush. She must have been startled when they disappeared, and I was mortified. As far as I could recall, I'd not been seen, even by my husband, without eyebrows penciled in for more than thirty years.

In those thirty years, I didn't swim under water, despite my love of swimming; I always found a way to keep my head out. Taking the kids to water parks when they were younger was easy because they liked water slides and splashing pools, but I was careful not to let them splash my face. Taking them to the community pool when they were older was a bit trickier, but I think I managed pretty successfully to keep my head above water. It became second nature to protect my eyes—to protect my penciled eyebrows—at all cost, through college and swimming with friends when I was single, through getting married, having kids, and watching those kids grow up. I was hobbled by my refusal to get my face wet because of the damn eyebrows—because of OCD that I never allowed myself to acknowledge, discuss, or treat.

I carried an eyebrow pencil like other women carried lip gloss, or like men carry a wallet; I always had one with me.

It didn't do any good that night, though. When I was finally released, encased in a heavy cast and shivering under the blanket around my shoulders, I was transported in my wheelchair back through the

ER and past reception—with no eyebrows. I got in the car and rested my arm on a pillow as my husband drove me home—with no eyebrows. It was the most emotionally excruciating hour of my life. No amount of pain medication was going to dull the humiliation of being exposed. And the next day, I remember thinking, This has got to stop.

MY BOYFRIEND ASKED ME TO MARRY HIM ON A ROMANTIC CHRISTMAS MORNING BY A ROARING FIRE.

He also bought me a piano, because my old upright didn't fit through his door, and a golf cart just for kicks. We started planning our wedding for the following fall because I'd always envisioned a crisp, cool, fall wedding that would not involve a lot of sweat. It simply hadn't occurred to me that it would be any other way, and, by God, it wouldn't.

Two months after getting engaged, I got the phone call I knew would one day come: The ex-boyfriend was in the hospital. His brother was telling people he had brain cancer, and, of course, I went along with it. After all those years, I went right back to being the lying, deceiving, guilt-ridden girl I used to be—protecting him.

I went to see him at the hospital, and he already looked dead. He'd gone from his robust 170 pounds to about 120, and there were just sticks where his legs used to be. He'd aged forty years in the nine years since his diagnosis, and something told me he never did start taking care of himself.

I started crying when I walked in the room and saw him, and he said, "Aw, Mag, don't. We always knew the bug was gonna get me."

I pulled myself together and sat on the side of his bed. "Does it hurt?" I asked.

"No," he said, "not really. They're giving me some pretty good drugs." And he tried to laugh, knowing I'd appreciate the humor in his response. I smiled, because I did, but that was about the best I could do.

"How're you doing?" he asked me after a few moments. It seemed neither of us could find our tongues.

"I'm good," I said. "I'm getting married in the fall. Finally, huh?" I managed a smile.

He did, too. "Glad to hear it. I always hoped you'd be happy."

I wanted to say, *And I always hoped you'd tell me how in God's name you got this*, but what came out was, "I always hoped you knew that I loved you."

He squeezed my hand, and at that moment another friend came to visit. I said good-bye and that I'd visit again, and made it out the door of the hospital before I began sobbing—sobbing for him, for me, for everything that used to be but was no more. Sobbing for how he hurt me, how he killed a part of me even if he hadn't given me the virus, and sobbing for how sad I felt for him, dying like an old man when he wasn't an old man at all. Sobbing for the love and sense of belonging I'd had with him, that I'd never had before or since, which he'd destroyed— which we had destroyed together—which, in fact, needed to be destroyed if I was ever to have a healthy, loving relationship.

And I did find that healthy, loving relationship. We were married on a gorgeous fall afternoon surrounded by friends and family who, I think, were simply thrilled that it was finally happening, for both of us. The carnage that had become my face in the weeks leading up to the wedding was masked with professional makeup because the stress had kicked my OCD into full bloom. We honeymooned in the Caribbean, and, for ten days, I did not go underwater.

UNTIL YOU'RE A PARENT YOURSELF, YOU CAN'T REALLY SEE THE TOTAL IMPACT OF GROWING UP.

Especially, it seems, when an addicted parent and mental issues are involved. But even if you try to understand—do all of the reading, identify all of your baggage—there are some parts that come back to haunt you after you have kids of your own: leftover issues that you simply couldn't have addressed in advance because they're not exposed until you have kids. Or maybe it seems that way because, until you have kids of your own, you can simply pretend your own childhood was normal. Once your own kids come, you can't do that anymore because pretty much every single thing you do and say passes first through that filter in your mind that always tried to screen for what a normal response would have been in any given situation. And the only way you know how to find it is to remember.

When my child would drop something or break something, my very first thoughts were, How would a typical parent handle this? And how would a typical child handle this? I would think back to my own childhood, reflexively, and remember how things were handled, and decide, in those few seconds while my children awaited my reaction, whether those ways were helpful. Not unlike any new parent in any given generation, I was trying to find the best way to parent with the tools I had and the only basis for comparison that I knew: How would I have preferred my parents to handle this kind of situation, and how would I have preferred to handle it myself? Everything is a function of these simple questions: How did I feel as a kid when that happened? How *should* a kid feel when that happens?

I've always just wanted so desperately to be normal. It's as simple and, actually, as complicated as that because you can ask twenty different people what "normal" is and get twenty different responses. And yet almost everything I've ever done in my life has been driven by that need. When I finished school early to get a jump on life, I thought, this is it. Now I can start over and be happy. When I quit bartending and started working at the law firm, I thought, this is it. Now I can start over and be happy. When I quit drinking, I thought the same thing. When I joined karate, finished grad school, and met my husband, each time, I thought—again—this is it. Now I can start over and be happy. And every single time, the demon caught up with me: the demon that is my mind, that is the OCD that I could not fix because I could not acknowledge it, because I didn't know what it was.

Then I had children and thought, no, this is the cure: the unconditional and absolute love of these little people for me, no matter my flaws. I'd discovered the cure for this cancer of my mind, I was sure of it. This is the end of the rainbow. And again, beyond rational thought, it wasn't.

I tried to ignore the shadow of doubt that continually nagged at the back of my mind: the one that reminded me that I hadn't yet fixed the flaw in the system. I was successful for just-long-enough periods of time to think that I had, until the old, familiar pangs of self-doubt and self-disgust resurfaced with such force as my kids grew older that ignoring them would take more effort than embracing them. So, this was my epiphany.

The problem is me, and it is inside, not outside. If the problem is inside, then the solution must also be inside. And it is not finding the elusive Prince Charming, or having the perfect parents or a sober father. It is finding me; I'm the one I've been searching for all of this time. There is something about me that I don't understand, have never understood, and have spent way too much of my life pretending I don't need to understand in order to be happy. And as long as I don't know what's wrong—or know but don't talk about it—I will continue searching and I will continue to hide my issues in shame.

I also needed to let go of my steadfast belief that mental diseases and disorders don't happen to intelligent, successful people; I blame this limiting belief for much of my inability through the years to recognize that I needed help. And, of course, that paradigm is ridiculous; mental diseases and mental illness don't discriminate any more than physical diseases do. The discrimination comes about when people who have mental disorders are made to feel ashamed of them because of fear and lack of communication. And then it's not the disease doing the discriminating.

I needed to admit to myself that I was still often compelled to pick and pluck. And that even after fifteen years of marriage and two children, losing a few pounds—for any reason, including having the flu—prompted me to starve myself so I could lose more. The obsessive thought was always right below the surface, awaiting an invitation. And it came down to whether that invitation was extended or not.

I KNEW AT LEAST PART OF THE ANSWERS I SOUGHT WERE GOING TO BE FOUND IN MY CHILDHOOD.

Six or seven years ago, in an effort to jog some memories when I started writing all of this down, I started driving by my old house with the barn every time I went home to see my parents. My family hasn't lived there for thirty years, and yet seeing it again brings both a comfort and an agony that makes me want to be twelve again so badly that I physically ache. I've never lost the fantasy of going back to childhood and having a chance to do it again, to be happy this time.

When I first started going back, I would drive very slowly past the place and then turn around down the road a bit and drive slowly back. I was trying to remember what my life there had felt like and couldn't; all I had were photographs in my mind.

Eventually, I just parked out in front and hoped to God no one called the police; I would just sit and stare, trying to conjure up those years that were, in their absence, causing me such grief. But even that wasn't enough, and one day I found myself walking up to a man pulling weeds next to the shed. I explained who I was, and we were both thrilled to realize that he remembered my family. His family had owned the farm for twenty-five years or so, he said, and he welcomed me to look around. I didn't even know where to start.

I went from the shed to the garage to the stable, taking it all in and pairing images with the picture frames in my head as I passed through them. I lingered at the place where the big barn gate used to be, envisioning the horses hanging their heads over it in search of sugar cubes from our hands. Then I moved on.

I walked into the barn and inhaled. Immediately, I got light-headed and started, in true panic-attack form, to hyperventilate; the sensations were overpowering and not just to my nose. The hay, the lingering smell of the manure, the loft, the thickness of the air—all threatened to suffocate me. I came out sobbing for everything that used to be but is no more: the childhood I couldn't do over and the parents who couldn't do their part over either. What a cruel irony, I remember thinking; I came back looking for validation for how screwed up I am, and what I've realized instead is how hard it was for all of us. Not just for me. Not just for my siblings. For all of us.

I headed down to the pond to try to collect myself, only to be overwhelmed by the sights and smells of the field, the water, the stream, the pasture. I had an overwhelming sense of desperation, of grief, of frustration, of fear, of sadness. Maybe when there aren't enough acceptable ways to turn these feelings outward, we learn to turn them inward instead. They have to go somewhere, right? Otherwise, our heads would explode.

OCD tormented me long before I was old enough to understand what it was: a quantifiable, recognized mental disorder. I was aware enough to know something was wrong with me, and I believed for whatever reasons that I couldn't discuss it, and I internalized the attendant shame long before I was old enough to understand what that was. Because the obsessive thoughts and corresponding rituals—which weren't always present, making it even more confusing—changed and morphed and evolved and devolved through the years, there was little continuity for me to focus on, even if I wanted to try to define what was wrong. There were always new kinds of crazy popping up, leading me to the "lightning rod" self-image that haunted me all of these years. I had no way of knowing that almost all of those bad things were, in fact, one thing—one thing that other people had, too: a thing that could actually be helped with therapy and anti-anxiety medications, and that did not, in fact, have to rule my life.

I grew up believing I was different in a bad way, and, while I would not change a thing about my life as it is now, if I'd known at ten or twenty—or forty even—what I know now, I know my life would not have been nearly as painful and shameful and lonely.

I FINALLY WENT TO A DERMATOLOGIST FOR MY "ADULT ACNE" IN MY LATE THIRTIES.

I was the mother of two young children. He was a pompous, arrogant man who did not address me but rather dictated his notes as he was examining me. This made it quite awkward to ask a question, and it gave me the sense at all times that he wasn't aware I was listening. He told me he needed to remove two or three pre-cancers from my face, scowled as he asked about my history of sun exposure, and proceeded to zap me not two or three but nineteen times with liquid nitrogen. He then had the nerve to ask me how long I'd been "scratching" at my acne.

"Oh, I don't know—I guess about, oh, thirty years or so . . . ," I answered, tears stinging my nitrogen-burned skin. What I wanted to say, but couldn't, was, "How long have you had trouble with math? You said 'two or three'!" And then I wanted to follow it up with, "How long have you had such a successful bedside manner?" But I've never been able to say things like this because it could make someone mad. That's never left me either.

"Well, stop doing it," he said, ignoring my crying. "Picking at your skin makes it difficult to see potential problems." He then went back to dictating around me, while I sat there fuming. What I wanted to say, but couldn't, again, was something like this: "Oh, stop? That's all there was to it all this time? I just needed some horse's ass to tell me to stop, and that would be the end of it? Oh, my God! All this time! And I just needed you to tell me to stop? You stupid, arrogant, son of a bitch." "Just stop," he says. Like I can.

I went to a different dermatologist after that, one who took a slightly different approach. Whether or not she knew why I did what I did, she figured out that I truly couldn't stop and put me on drugs to stop the acne, which left me with nothing on my face to pick at. Problem solved—at least on their end.

I've been to many different doctors in recent years, as a matter of fact. After my kids were born and I realized what it felt like to want to live, I spent many hours at many doctors' offices making sure I had done no permanent damage to my body in my pre-children, pre-wanting-to-live days. My OCD still convinces me on a daily basis of my imminent demise, and I admit to spending hours on the Internet sometimes, researching my symptoms and assigning various fatal diseases to them. Yes, I know I'm a hypochondriac, but guess what? Even hypochondriacs eventually get sick. And I'll be ready.

I DO HAVE A GOOD LIFE NOW.

It will never be a perfect life, but it is far better than it certainly could have been, given some of the choices I made along the way. Fortunately, in spurts of sanity, I often managed to propel myself one step farther up from the bottom of the pit, one step closer to full-time light. The exertion, of course, would force me to "rest" for varying amounts of time, but then, one day, it would happen again; I would somehow muster the energy to submit a resume, or enter recovery, or join karate, or find a better place to live. And I'd be a step closer to normal, yet again.

Even though it's not perfect, it's close enough to perfect in all the ways it needs to be; I know I can live with the struggles because I've done it all of my life. I do the best I can with my kids, in terms of being fair and honest and never giving them reason to doubt my love for them. I try to do the same with my husband, although sometimes I go out of bounds with my need for love and attention, and he tries his best to understand the reasons behind it.

I've always tried to control my sarcasm around my family because, even though my husband accepts it as the defense mechanism it is, I can't expect my children to understand. And it often comes out when I'm frustrated or angry, which is not how I want my kids to learn to manage those emotions. I've been reasonably successful, I think; while both of my children demonstrated a gift for humor at an embarrassingly young age, their sarcasm is without anger. It is simply an appreciation of irony.

My dad and I have a great relationship these days. He's still everything he used to be—opinionated, passionate, somewhat loud-voiced—but without the alcohol. He is something of an extreme couponer; his indulgence of this quirk enables him each month to buy bulk toiletries that he then donates to homeless shelters. My mom is, in her mid-seventies, a certified lifeguard, and my dad is her helper. And on the morning of 9/11, as I sat in front of my TV watching the end of the world as I knew it, he's the one I called. I needed him to make some sense of it, reassure me somehow, and tell me if I should go get my son from preschool—because he is my father.

The OCD, of course, never goes away permanently, but it does take sabbaticals on occasion. I trim my nails from time to time, in an effort to stop plucking, like how I used the Band-Aids to help me quit sucking my thumb. Sometimes it works for months at a time and I think I'm finally over it, but then I'll be watching television one night and, before I know it, they're all gone— eyebrows and eyelashes alike. I start over the next day, trimming my nails, and it's like those months in between never happened.

I watch my weight, although I don't weigh myself four and five times a day anymore. My pregnancies were challenging, to put it mildly; I gained sixty-five pounds with each child—no easy trick, considering I actually lost ten pounds the first five months of my second pregnancy—and it took a supreme effort each day to eat well and put the best interests of the babies first. I realize how ridiculous this must sound to someone who doesn't have this problem, particularly when we're talking about the miracle of pregnancy and childbirth. But just as knowing I'm too thin can make me euphoric, gaining weight, for whatever reason, can send me plummeting into a depression from which it could take months to recover. It's not logical; it's just the way it is.

I take antidepressants for the mood swings and anxiety attacks, and they seem to do the trick. I call them my "happy pills," and I keep waiting for the "self-confidence pills" and "self-esteem pills" to come on the market—although I know, on some level, that the OCD is what caused those deficits in me in the first place, and that they may not be entirely recoverable. I also know that there's a hereditary tendency for many of these mental disorders and, fortunately for my kids, what to look for in them. That—my knowledge—I can give them.

EPILOGUE

2014, AGE FIFTY-TWO.

"So why are you doing this?"

This is a question I've asked myself and have been asked by people who care about me, for several years now. Why am I putting myself out there, exposing the embarrassment and shame of a lifetime that I spent years in therapy trying to heal? Things in my life are really good now, so why am I bringing all this up?

I'm bringing it up because I understand now what OCD is, and I know what it can do when left unacknowledged. The effect of this mental disorder on my self-esteem was catastrophic, and the majority of my life has been spent in search, first, of "What's wrong with me?" and next, of "Can I be fixed?" I also know that, like addiction and anxiety, the tendency toward it can be hereditary. As I watched my daughter start to struggle with the initial manifestations of OCD a few years ago, before adolescence even, I thought, enough. This stops here. Not the OCD—because, while it can be managed, right now it can't really be cured—but the fear and the shame and the inability to talk about what's happening to her. If she's going to wrestle with this, she's going to wrestle it with knowledge, self-confidence, understanding from others, and the safety of knowing that it's just a thing that she has—and that *she* can control *it*, rather than the other way around.

Sir Francis Bacon said that knowledge is power. Knowledge about mental illness can change an otherwise debilitating and shameful facet of a child's life into an element of her personality that simply needs to be managed, much like near-sightedness or flat feet. If a child is encouraged to communicate and to ask for help, and taught to be self-aware and self-accepting, then two things could happen: The child's self-esteem won't be destroyed, and the perception of mental illness, both internal and external, can change.

If you know that you do something over and over and that the repetition is something you want to stop but can't, then you should be able to say—to your parents or your teachers or your friends or your spouse—"Hey, I think I've got something going on in my head that I'd like to get a handle on. Can you help me?" It should be as easy as that. We have no problem saying, "Hey, I think I sprained my wrist; can you take me to a doctor?" Telling someone we need mental help should be that easy, that straightforward, that judgment-free.

Too much of my behavior—my rituals and thoughts—are steeped in blame and shrouded in shame. I never allowed myself to share any of them with the people I knew and loved because I was ashamed of them; I still am, in some cases. I went through way too much, for way too long, completely alone because behaviors associated with OCD can be about as isolating as it gets. And now that I know this, I'd like to stop it, thank you. I can't stop the disorder, but, if I can talk about it and if my children can talk about it, then maybe we can stop the loss of self-esteem that can take a lifetime to recover.

One day I was unexpectedly drawn into a conversation with my then seven-year-old son about my alcoholism. I'd always intended to tell my kids when they were older, but circumstances in this moment dictated that he and I have the discussion sooner rather than later. Afterward, I wrote a column about the conversation:

I keep my cleaning supplies locked in a cabinet under the kitchen sink. I thought that keeping them hidden would protect my kids—that if I showed them where and what they were, they'd be more inclined to want to experiment with them and would get hurt. If they didn't know the stuff was there, then there wouldn't be any danger.

Of all people, I should know that pretending something doesn't exist doesn't make it so.

My son and I were reading a book together. It was one that might have been a little mature for some seven-year-olds, but we've been reading novels for so long already that I didn't give it a second thought. As we got further into the book, I realized one of the main characters had a drinking problem, although it wasn't being addressed directly.

It wasn't, at least, until the last chapter. It became clear then that the character's alcoholism was the central issue behind his actions, and his actions were the central issue of the story.

My son asked me what that meant, and I explained it the best I could on short notice. I told him that some people have a physical problem with alcohol, while others don't; that people with this problem have a very hard time not drinking, but that not drinking is the only way to be okay. Unfortunately, some people aren't able to quit, and it can affect their lives—and the lives of people they love—in a bad way.

He responded, "Alcoholics must be bad people then."

And there it was. I was blindsided. I always knew we would have this conversation one day because, from the generations of alcoholics before me, I am keenly aware of the damage that comes from not talking about it. But I thought he'd be a little older—and that I'd be a little more prepared.

"Oh, no, honey," I said, "Alcoholics aren't bad people. It's a disease, and people with this disease just have to make sure they don't drink."

"But the guy in the book did bad things," he persisted.

"Maybe," I said, "but he was not a bad person." I was stalling, trying to put off the inevitable as long as I could. But I simply could not let him walk away from this conversation with the very belief system I wanted to dispel. I could not perpetuate the cycle of guilt and shame of which I'd been a victim all of my life.

"You know," I then said, "Mommy's an alcoholic."

His face took on a look of confusion and fright. "But . . . are you sick?" he asked.

"No, sweetie, I'm not sick. I've been sober for fifteen years. I'm what they call a 'recovering alcoholic.' I was able to get help a long time ago, before you were born, before I even met Daddy. I knew I had to get better if I ever wanted to have you all in my life someday."

He mulled this over for a few moments and asked, "Will I be an alcoholic?"

Once again I was not prepared for the question. The truth is that, based on my family history, there's a chance he may have a problem with drinking—

but he's certainly too young to adopt that worry. Still, I chose not to lie—a choice that was more difficult than I care to admit.

"I don't know," I finally said, "but I do know that whatever challenges you face when you get older, Daddy and I will help you through them. That's why we talk about things—so that you'll always be able to come to us." That satisfied him, and I thought this was the end of it.

It wasn't. He came home from school a few days later, put down his backpack, and said, "Hi, Mom! Um . . . you were drunk, weren't you?"

Wiping the initial shock off my face, I replied, "Well, yes, I guess I was. I mean, well . . . why do you ask, honey?"

He pulled out a paper from school that explained the workings of the lungs, with a section on the ill effects of smoking.

"The teacher said that we shouldn't smoke because it's addictive, and once you start, sometimes you can't stop. And I raised my hand and said, 'That's like my mom with drinking!'" He was so proud of himself for making that connection and, yet, in need of some reassurance that it was okay to do so.

I stood there silently, trying to picture his classmates' dinner conversations that night. I was imagining his party invitations drying up and play dates dwindling away, when suddenly I caught myself. I was doing exactly what I did when I was a kid, and exactly what I didn't want my kids to do: I was letting myself be ashamed.

And in that moment, with my son waiting expectantly for some clue that he hadn't done anything wrong, I knew what I had to say and I knew I had to be ready to live it. I kissed his head and said, "Yes, honey. That's right. They're very similar." He smiled and walked away, presumably filing the information away in his head under "Things to Know Later." And he taught me something in the process.

The mere existence of something does not make it dangerous. What makes it dangerous is not understanding what it is and what it can do, which leads to judgment and fear and prejudice. Knowledge, I'm learning, truly is power, and so I'm going to go get my children and head for the kitchen.

We've got some cabinets to unlock.

AT THE TIME THIS COLUMN WAS PUBLISHED, I WAS ASKED THE SAME QUESTION: "WHY?"

Why write about it? Why disclose it? Why do this to yourself?

The answer then was easy. I did it because I needed to start breaking the cycle of shame associated with addiction. I needed to clarify it for my son before he had an opportunity to adopt the hand-me-down theme of embarrassment and shame. And I was glad I did it—until I realized later that alcoholism was not the only secret I harbored. There were more that had to be exorcised, and writing is my priest.

Suddenly, I was teetering on a fence between my past and my future—and my kids' futures. My past secrets—and present, for that matter—may well affect their futures. Will they be surprised to read this book and learn some things about Mommy that she doesn't really talk about? Possibly, but, then again, maybe I'll be able to talk about them more easily now. Will they be more equipped to handle their own issues if they know it's okay to talk about them and get help for them? I hope so. Will they still love me? Without a doubt.

If I really wanted to break the cycle of shame and guilt that seems endemic to people like me—who seem to have perfectly normal, happy lives while praying that, in the next moment, they won't have to count, pluck, use, or pick—and if I wanted to be honest with my children, my husband, my family, and my friends, then I had to be honest with myself. The paradox has always been that I can't be honest if I'm ashamed, yet the shame has always shrouded the honesty. It's time to break through the shroud.

And, most importantly, this is for my kids and any other kids who grow up with these kinds of issues and concerns and fears. I want them to be able to talk about them openly and honestly, without blame and without shame, like people talk about acne and periods and break-ups. I don't want them to spend half their lives in their rooms, hurting and wondering why they're always so alone. I want to empower them on their journey through life—from the innocence of white belt to the enlightenment of black—to fight back.

That's why I'm doing this.

RESOURCES

Adult Children of Alcoholics
Mailing address:
ACA WSO, P.O. Box 3216
Torrance, CA 90510

Phone: 562-595-7831

Web: www.adultchildren.org

Beyond OCD and OCD Education Station
2300 Lincoln Park West, Suite 206B
Chicago, IL 60614

Phone: 773-661-9530

Fax: 773-661-9535

Web: www.BeyondOCD.org and
www.OCDEducationStation.org

Children's and Adult Center for OCD and Anxiety

3138 Butler Pike, Suite 200
Plymouth Meeting, PA 19462

Phone: 484-530-0778, ext. 8

Fax: 484-530-0998

Web: www.WorryWiseKids.org

International OCD Foundation, Inc.

Mailing address:
P.O. Box 961029
Boston, MA 02196

Physical address:
18 Tremont Street, Suite 903
Boston, MA 02108

Phone: 617-973-5801

Fax: 617-973-5803

Email: info@iocdf.org

Web: www.iocdf.org

Massachusetts General Hospital: OCD and Related Disorders Program

Richard B. Simches Research Center

185 Cambridge Street, Suite 2000
Boston, MA 02114

Phone: 617-726-6766

Web: www.mghocd.org

Web (support for families):
www.OCDandFamilies.org

National Association for Children of Alcoholics
Mailing Address:
NACoA, 10920 Connecticut Ave, Suite 100
Kensington, MD 20895

Phone: 888-55-4COAS or 301-468-0985

Fax: 301-468-0987

Email: nacoa@nacoa.org

Web: http://www.nacoa.org/